GCSE

cess

GUIDE

4|12
I|13

HAR

nguage
ature

Emma Owen
Paul Burns

Contents

Drama

Revised

Prose

Revised

Poetry

Revised

Speaking and Listening

Revised

Course Overview

Introduction

This book is designed to help you during your study of GCSE English or GCSE English Language and GCSE English Literature. It covers all of the sections you will study as part of your controlled assessments and exam preparation. It will also look at the skills you need for reading, writing, speaking and listening.

In GCSE English Language and GCSE English Literature there are many occasions when there is no right or wrong answer.

Teachers and examiners are looking for responses that are well structured and grammatically correct, and demonstrate your ability to communicate clearly. However, your interpretation of the texts that you study is personal and what you might see, somebody else might not. As long as you can justify your response and back up what you say with evidence from the text, you are on the right track.

GCSEs in English

All exam boards offer GCSE English – you could study just GCSE English, which is a combination of Language and Literature; or you could do dual entry GCSE English Language and English Literature.

The GCSE English course requires you to study three core elements – Reading, Writing and Speaking and Listening. The GCSE in English Language, which is taught alongside GCSE English Literature, also requires you to look at these three main areas. For both English and English Language, candidates are required to complete a Spoken Language Study. Some of the work that you do as part of your GCSE English Language will also contribute to the mark that you get for GCSE English Literature.

GCSE English Literature will expand your Language skills – you will study a range of texts and then produce responses to these. Over the duration of the course you will study:
- a play by William Shakespeare
- a range of poetry – both poetry from the English literary heritage and poetry that has been written more recently
- a modern play
- prose from the English literary heritage and prose that has been written more recently – usually novels or short stories, but sometimes non-fiction.

The texts that you study will depend on your school. You will be asked to look at some texts individually and you will also be asked to compare texts. Some exam boards will allow you to compare your Shakespeare text to a film version, and some will allow you to produce a multi-modal response to Shakespeare.

Controlled Assessment

The work that you do for controlled assessments is assessed by your teachers and will contribute to your final mark. You will study a topic in class and your teacher will prepare you for the controlled assessment task, which will take place over several hours under exam conditions.

This book will help you to revise key areas that might come up in controlled assessment tasks. Unlike in exams, in controlled assessment you will have access to notes which you have prepared in advance.

In addition to knowing the content well it is important that you familiarise yourself with exam technique. Where possible you should try to look at past papers so that you know what type of questions will be asked and what skills are required.

When you are in the exam, in order to help you understand what the question is asking, you can underline or highlight key words. Some questions will require a long response and for these it is useful to make a quick plan. Make sure that you read through your responses when you have written them, checking your answers for mistakes.

For GCSE English Language and GCSE English Literature you will be required to demonstrate a number of different skills:

- **Creative or imaginative writing** – some questions will ask for a creative or imaginative response. As well as being able to demonstrate your flair, it is important to show your grammatical skill and technical accuracy.

- **Functional writing** – some writing questions will ask you to demonstrate the skills you might use in more 'everyday' writing, such as letters, reports or information leaflets. Here you can show your awareness of purpose and audience, as well as your technical skills.

- **Analysis of written texts** – this type of question could require you to analyse a poem that you have studied in class, an extract from a novel or an unseen non-fiction text. You must make sure that you focus on what the question asks you to do and pick out key elements, whether these are literary techniques or presentational devices. You then need to explain the effect that these elements have on you as a reader. You will need to reinforce the points that you make with quotations or evidence from the texts.

- **Comparative responses** – you need to explore all aspects of your texts while keeping focus on the question. Consider both similarities and differences. Make sure that you give a personal response to the texts.

Revision Tips

Some people find that revising for English Language and Literature is difficult; however, there are lots of things that you can do to prepare. The best place to start is to read. Look again at any texts that you have studied in class: the more familiar you are with these the easier it will be to write about them. Know your texts in detail and have plenty of ideas about them. Make sure that you can cover a range of points, supporting them with accurate references to texts. Reading for pleasure is also important – the better read you are the more vivid your imagination is and the more extensive your vocabulary will be. Look at the list below for more specific ways to revise:

- Brainstorm and create a bank of possible exam questions on a given text/collection of poems.
- Traffic light code each of these questions according to how confidently you think you could answer them; use green for confidently, orange for quite confidently and red for not confidently.

- Look at possible exam/controlled assessment style questions and plan your responses.
- Make a list of quotations that you think are important.
- Make posters and visual aids to help you remember key terms/ideas/themes in texts.
- Create word banks for different topics – make sure that you know how to spell these words correctly and understand their meanings.
- Use your revision guide to consolidate your understanding.

Back to Basics

How to do Well in English

The content of your exams and controlled assessments will vary slightly depending on the exam board you are with. However, certain things will be the same for everyone. Making sure that your work is technically accurate is vital.

Errors in spelling, punctuation and grammar can make your work difficult to understand and even change its meaning.

Punctuation

Punctuating your writing correctly and effectively is much more than just using a full stop at the end of a sentence.

- Are you familiar with the different types of punctuation shown here?
- How many different types of punctuation do you use in your writing?
- Can you understand why different forms of punctuation are more effective than others?

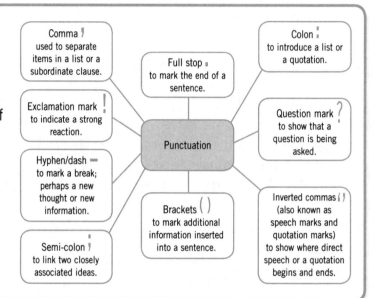

Comma ,
used to separate items in a list or a subordinate clause.

Full stop .
to mark the end of a sentence.

Colon :
to introduce a list or a quotation.

Exclamation mark !
to indicate a strong reaction.

Punctuation

Question mark ?
to show that a question is being asked.

Hyphen/dash —
to mark a break; perhaps a new thought or new information.

Brackets ( )
to mark additional information inserted into a sentence.

Inverted commas ' '
(also known as speech marks and quotation marks) to show where direct speech or a quotation begins and ends.

Semi-colon ;
to link two closely associated ideas.

Paragraphs

Another basic element of any writing is making sure that you have used paragraphs correctly. Look at the boxes below for a brief guide to the rules of paragraphing.

These are just the basics – as we look at elements of GCSE English Language and English Literature in more detail, we will focus on how we can use the basics to take our writing to a higher level.

Change of time, for example:
   ...He was dead to the world.
   Days had passed before he woke from his deep sleep.

Paragraphs are used to show that a new point is being made, or that there is a change of situation or topic.

Change of person, for example:
   In spite of all her undoubtedly admirable qualities, I could never really warm to Mrs Pinchberry.
   With Mr Pinchberry, on the other hand, things were completely different.

Change of speaker, for example:
   'And what's more, don't you ever speak to me like that again!' Mana shouted as she flounced out of the room.
   'I'll speak to you however I like,' I mumbled meekly.

Change of topic, for example:
   Whether it is because of this fierce independence or in spite of it, millions of people would find their lives poorer without a pet cat.
   While they share many of the traits of their domesticated cousins, 'big cats' demonstrate some behaviours which are quite different.

Change of place, for example:
   And so we watched as the strange creatures disappeared into the forest from which they had emerged so unexpectedly.
   Unknown to us, in the castle a huge banquet was being prepared in our honour.

Capital Letters

It is important that you use capital letters correctly. Look at the illustration below to check that you know when and where to use capital letters. Many of the examples given are proper nouns – nouns which name a particular person or thing and which always start with a capital letter.

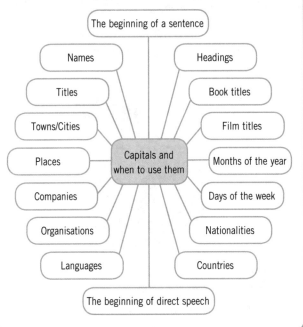

The beginning of a sentence

Names

Titles

Towns/Cities

Places

Companies

Organisations

Languages

Headings

Book titles

Film titles

Months of the year

Days of the week

Nationalities

Countries

Capitals and when to use them

The beginning of direct speech

Sentences

Using a variety of sentences is a key part of demonstrating your ability to craft your writing and create certain effects. However, the most important part is making sure that your sentences are grammatically correct.

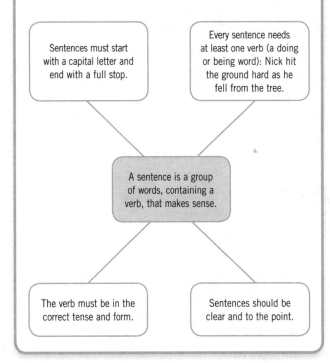

Sentences must start with a capital letter and end with a full stop.

Every sentence needs at least one verb (a doing or being word): Nick hit the ground hard as he fell from the tree.

A sentence is a group of words, containing a verb, that makes sense.

The verb must be in the correct tense and form.

Sentences should be clear and to the point.

❓ Test Yourself

1 When and where should you use capital letters?

2 What are the main types of punctuation?

3 What are the main rules of writing a grammatically correct sentence?

4 What are the basic rules of paragraphing?

⭐ Stretch Yourself

1 The following text has not been divided into paragraphs. Put it in paragraphs, adding appropriate linking phrases or connectives.

On behalf of the students of Ash Meadow, I would like to share with you our concerns about the school environment. When I say 'environment' I mean not the state of the world in general, but the surroundings in which we all work. We students have become very concerned about the amount of litter in the school. The corridors and classrooms are covered in all kinds of detritus: sweet wrappers, empty crisp packets and discarded drink cans. Desks are covered in offensive graffiti and their undersides studded with stale gum. In the corridors very few bins are provided and they are overflowing with litter. They are too small and too flimsy for the job.

Again, there is graffiti. Our beautiful displays, into which we have put so much work, have been violated and defaced. This will not motivate the students of Ash Meadow. I turn to the foyer – the first impression given to any visitor. Not the warmest of welcomes. It is drab, uncared for and unfriendly. No one entering it would feel welcome. No one could leave it without a sense of relief. I should be most grateful if you, as Principal of Ash Meadow College, would give my points some thought. We, the students, would be only too happy to present you with our own proposals for improvement.

Writing Skills

Writing Skills

In both exams and controlled assessments, you will be required to demonstrate your writing skills. You will have a variety of tasks to choose from.

The type of question you are asked will vary according to your exam board, but all your answers should have certain common features. You must show that you can:

- write clearly and imaginatively
- understand who the intended audience is
- use a variety of formats, for example letter / speech / article
- structure your text – it needs to have a beginning, middle and an end
- use paragraphs to organise your writing for effect
- use a variety of sentences, punctuation and vocabulary to show flair and creativity
- maintain an appropriate voice and tone throughout
- use Standard English and correctly spelt words.

⚟ Boost Your Memory

Use the following mnemonic as a checklist to make sure you have considered everything:

A – Audience
P – Purpose / Presentation
P – Paragraphs / Punctuation
L – Language
E – Effects
S – Sentences and Spellings

Audience

The intended audience for your text will determine the type of language that you use as well as the content of your writing. It is important that you always ask yourself the question: is what you have written suitable for your intended audience? For example, if you were asked to write a letter to your school's governors, you would have to lay it out and address it appropriately, using formal language throughout.

A blog for teenagers would have a completely different layout, using eye-catching presentational devices and much less formal language.

✓ Maximise Your Marks

Knowing about and understanding different types of audience will help you gain higher marks. Among the aspects of your audience you might consider are age, gender, social class, interests, background, culture and your relationship with the audience. Think about what kind of vocabulary you would use and whether the general tone of your writing would be formal or informal.

Purpose and Presentation

One of the first things you consider is the purpose of your writing. This will be made clear in your question. Possible purposes include:
- to inform
- to explain
- to persuade
- to advise
- to entertain
- to describe.

Once you know what type of writing it is that you are being asked to produce, make sure that you think about layout and presentation. If you are being asked to write a magazine article to persuade teenagers to revise, then be inspired by the conventions and have an interesting heading and subheading, etc. You should not, however, write in columns or include illustrations.

Punctuation

To achieve good marks in any piece of work, you have to use a range of punctuation. This means more than full stops and capital letters. For a good mark you must demonstrate that you can also use commas, question marks and inverted commas correctly and effectively. An A* candidate will also be able to use colons, semi-colons and dashes effectively.

Language

The language that you use needs to be appropriate for your audience – most writing tasks will require you to use Standard English. Just as you might alter the way you speak according to the situation and your audience, so must you use written language that is appropriate to your audience, purpose and form. You should take into account vocabulary, grammar and language techniques.

Paragraphing

Paragraphing is about much more than indenting or leaving a line between sections of your writing – paragraphs are used to support and develop the meaning of your text. Effective paragraphs usually start with topic sentences and are linked by connective phrases or discourse markers. A discourse (or discursive) marker is a word or a phrase which shows the relationship between the new paragraph or sentence and the one before it. Below are some examples of words and phrases that you might use to link paragraphs and sentences.

Adding	Also, As well as, Moreover, Furthermore, In addition
Cause and effect	Consequently, Therefore, Thus
Sequencing	Firstly, Secondly, Then, Next, Meanwhile, After, Finally
Qualifying	However, Yet, But despite, As long as, Unless, Apart from
Emphasising	Notably, Significantly, In particular, Especially, Obviously, Clearly, Above all, Most importantly
Illustrating	In the case of, For example, As revealed by
Comparing	Likewise, Equally, Similarly, In the same way
Contrasting	In contrast, On the other hand, Unlike, Whereas, Alternatively
Temporal	Earlier, Later, Afterwards, Now

⚲ Boost Your Memory

To remember when to paragraph, look at the features below and structure your writing accordingly. We start a new paragraph each time we change:

TOPIC	PLACE	TIME	PERSON	SPEAKER

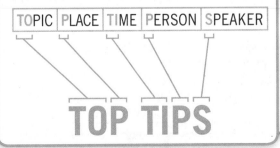

TOP TIPS

Writing Skills

Sentences

There are four main sentence types: simple, compound, complex and minor:

- A simple sentence must contain a subject (the person or thing doing the action) and a verb (the action). For example: *Emma sat the exam.*
- A compound sentence joins two or more clauses (phrases that could stand alone as simple sentences) together, using a conjunction such as 'and', 'but' or 'so'. For example: *Emma sat the exam and she answered all of the questions.*
- A complex sentence has two or more clauses joined together. The main clause should make sense by itself but the subordinate clause, which adds detail or explanation, will not. Conjunctions are not needed but

you might need to use a relative pronoun. For example: *Emma, never one to shirk a challenge, sat the exam.*

- A minor sentence (or fragment) is, in a way, not really a sentence at all because it does not have a main verb. It is often an answer or exclamation, for example: *Tomorrow* or *Oh my word!*

As well as using a variety of sentence types in your writing, you should also vary the way that you structure your sentences. Starting your sentences with an adverb can create tension and allow you to withhold important information until later. For example: *Anxiously, Emma made her way into the examination hall.*

Common Misspellings

A	B	C	D	E	F
Accommodation	Beautiful	Caught	Dear	Embarrass	February
Although	Beginning	Column	Decision	Enquire	Fortunately
Analyse	Believe	Chose	Demonstrate	Environment	Friend
Analysis	Business	Choose	Development	Evident	Fulfil
Argument			Difficulty	Example	
Audience			Disappear		
			Disappoint		

G	H	I	J	K	L
Great	Happening	Interesting	Jealous	Know	Lovely
Government	Heard	It's (It is)	Jewellery	Knowledge	
	Height	Its (Belonging to it)			

M	N	O	P	Q	R
Marriage	Necessary	Obvious	Peace	Quiet	Read
Meanwhile			Performance	Quite	Receive
Moreover			Persuade		Reference
			Physical		Remember
			Practice (noun)		
			Practise (verb)		

S	T	U	V	W	Y
Saturday	Their (Belonging to them)	Unfortunately	Vain	Wednesday	Yesterday
Scene	There (In that place)		Vein	Weird	Your (Belonging to you)
Separate	They're (They are)		Very	Were	You're (You are)
Sincerely	To			We're (We are)	
Strategy	Too			Where	
Surely	Two			Woman	
Surprise	Tomorrow			Women	

Effects

Be creative and show the readers rather than telling them – take them on a journey in your writing. This can be done by using the correct stylistic conventions for the type of writing that you are doing. If you have been asked to describe a beach scene, for example, use descriptive techniques such as powerful adjectives and images. For example:
'The golden sands were reminiscent of a supermarket on Christmas Eve; people covered every single grain of sand', is more effective than 'The beach was crowded'.

Build Your Understanding

It is important to have a plan before you start writing your written response. Begin by identifying key words in the question so that you know what the focus of your writing will be. For example:

Write a <u>letter</u> to your <u>headteacher</u> <u>persuading</u> him/her that the timings of the school day should be altered.

Then create a thought shower or list of all the things that you will include. Use the APPLES mnemonic from page 8 to check that you have considered everything.

❓ Test Yourself

1. Which connective phrases can be used to emphasise a key point?

2. A colon and semi-colon are considered to be advanced forms of punctuation; find out when and where you can use a colon or semi-colon in your writing.

⭐ Stretch Yourself

1. Some of the trickiest spellings to remember are homophones. For each of the following sentences, choose the correct spelling:
   a) Yet again, Lucinda was late for hockey practice/practise.
   b) I'm sorry, Miss. I really didn't no/know the answer.
   c) I couldn't decide weather/whether to answer question one or question two.
   d) He's always very well dressed but he can be incredibly vain/vane.
   e) Ipods are not aloud/allowed in the exam hall.
   f) Did you really wright/write all that?
   g) Tony passed/past nearly all his exams.
   h) I heard/herd it on the grapevine.
   i) She walked straight passed/past me without saying a word!
   j) I promise I will practice/practise my French verbs tonight.
   k) If we don't hurry up were/we're going to be late for the rehearsal.

Reading Non-Fiction

What is Non-Fiction?

Every day we are bombarded with examples of non-fiction texts. From the junk mail that we receive through our letterbox, which we swiftly throw into the recycling bin, to the newspaper that keeps us up to speed with the world we live in. From celebrity gossip to current affairs; tourist attractions to charity campaigns; their topics are wide-ranging and diverse.

Non-fiction texts are used for a variety of purposes: to inform, entertain, advise, explain, persuade and instruct. Some non-fiction texts are also referred to as 'media texts'. These include newspaper and magazine articles, websites, leaflets and posters. Examples of other non-fiction texts are textbooks, manuals, cook books, encyclopedias, biographies, travel writing, essays, diaries and menus.

When studying non-fiction texts it is important to remember that each text type has its own **conventions**. These are the features that help us to determine and recognise what type of text it is. These conventions can be examples of language, structure, layout and presentation. For example, a newspaper report will have a headline and be written in columns. A recipe will have a list of ingredients followed by instructions, using imperatives (see page 14). They are crafted to more effectively convey their message to their target audience.

Analysing Non-Fiction

When you are given non-fiction texts to look at and analyse, you will be given a range of questions to answer that demonstrate that you can read and understand the information that is in front of you. The responses that you write for each question will demonstrate skills such as your ability to:

- read the information and summarise it in your own words
- locate and exemplify key information from the text
- distinguish between fact and opinion
- read between the lines and show an understanding of implied meaning
- make inferences and deductions about the texts
- compare and contrast different texts, identifying similarities and differences
- recognise and understand the effect of linguistic features in the texts
- understand and explain the effect of presentational features and the way the text is structured.

Build Your Understanding

When analysing non-fiction text types, there are key questions that we can ask about the texts, for example:

Who – who is the intended audience of this piece? How has the text been created to appeal to that particular audience?

What – what type of non-fiction text is it? How do you know?

Where – where did this text appear? If it is an advertisement, what type of publication was it taken from?

When – when was the text written? Is its time of publication important when recognising the messages contained within the text?

How – how does the text work? What methods has the writer used to get the message across? How is language used? How are presentational devices used?

Why – why has this text been written? What is its purpose?

P.E.E. Method

When you are in the exam and you are writing a response to a non-fiction text question, it is important that you pick out details from the texts to reinforce the points that you are making. An effective way of doing this is by using the P.E.E. method – a three-point answer that will make your response structured and detailed.

POINT – your topic sentence. Try to include key words from the question.

EVIDENCE – this is an example from the text that builds on and supports the point that you have just made.

EXPLANATION – this is the tricky bit, but if you get it right and explain the evidence that you chose and comment on the effect of it, you will demonstrate that you have a secure understanding of non-fiction texts.

For example:

P The writer uses the first person plural several times:

E 'As a people we are sometimes far too tolerant...we really need to do something about this now.'

E In this way she identifies herself as being 'one of us', implying that she has the same concerns and worries as her reader.

✓ Maximise Your Marks

More sophisticated answers will embed quotations or references from the texts into their answers and use the example given to reinforce the points that they are making without necessarily using the P.E.E. structure in the way shown here. They may also give more than one possible explanation, picking up on details of the evidence that has been quoted.

❓ Test Yourself

1 Rearrange the following sentences into the correct order to make it a P.E.E. paragraph:

'97 per cent of students who revise thoroughly will achieve at least their predicted grade.'

The leaflet, aimed at parents and written by teachers, uses lots of facts and statistics to encourage parents to make their children revise.

As this is such a high percentage, parents will be convinced of the benefits of revision and insist their children attend revision classes.

⭐ Stretch Yourself

1 Re-read some practice essays you have done during the year and/or model answers that your teacher has given. As you read, highlight good examples of the use of P.E.E. and places where you have not used P.E.E. effectively. Which part of P.E.E. are you not doing properly? If it is 'evidence', try to find some appropriate evidence to back up your point. If it is 'explanation', rewrite your explanation.

Conventions and Features

Conventions

Writers of non-fiction texts use a range of methods to give us an insight into the purpose of the text and create particular effects.

The style of a text can be determined by vocabulary and sentence structure. It can be descriptive and elaborate; formal and impersonal; or colloquial and relaxed. The style then links with the **tone**, which is the mood of the text. The tone is important and will vary according to the type of text. For example, an encyclopedia or manual would probably be concise and impersonal whereas an article for a celebrity magazine might be friendly and light-hearted in tone.

Language Features

Adjective – a word used to describe a noun which adds more detail and helps to paint a picture in the reader's mind.

Adverb – a word used to describe a verb, often ending in 'ly', such as 'swiftly', 'anxiously'. These are used to add detail to the action.

Alliteration – when a series of words begin with the same consonant sound such as 'the west wind whistled wildly'.

Ambiguity – when a sentence or idea is unclear and could have more than one interpretation.

Anecdote – a short account of an interesting or humorous story, often used to reinforce a point being made.

Assonance – a subtle rhyming of an internal vowel sound, such as 'I lie by the side of my bride'.

Direct address – when a speaker or writer directly addresses another individual.

Emotive language – language that is used evocatively to trigger a response in the reader.

Figure of speech – an expression which should not be taken literally, such as 'pigs might fly', meaning not that there are pigs flying past your window but that something is probably untrue.

Formal language – language that is similar to Standard English and used in situations where it is not appropriate to be too conversational.

Hyperbole – exaggeration. For example, when the piece of writing states that something is 'the best'.

Imagery – when words are so descriptive that they paint a picture in your mind. Imagery is used to allow the reader to empathise or imagine the moment being described.

Imperative – a command or instruction, for example 'go away' or 'take three eggs'.

Informal language – conversational language that is spoken between people who are usually familiar with one another.

Interrogative – question.

Irony – when words are used to imply an opposite meaning, or sarcastic language that can be used to mock or convey scorn.

Metaphor – an image is created by implicitly comparing one thing to another, such as 'my brother is a monkey'.

Personification – when an inanimate object is given human qualities, for example 'the television stared at me across the room'.

Pun – word play, when words are organised in an amusing way to suggest another meaning.

Repetition – when words, phrases, ideas or sentences are used more than once – this can be used to highlight key issues and make important sections more memorable.

Rhetorical question – a question that does not require an answer, used to make the reader think about the possible answer and involve them in the text.

Simile – a comparison of one thing to another using the words 'like' or 'as', such as 'the raindrops fell like tears'.

Slogan – a memorable phrase, often used in advertising and associated with a company.

Symbols and symbolism – when an object is used to represent something important or an abstract idea, such as a heart being used to symbolise love or a dove being used to symbolise peace.

Non-Fiction

Presentational Devices

Bold font – when a heavier font has been used to draw attention to important sections.

Bullet points – typographical symbols used to introduce items in a list.

Caption – a title, short explanation or description accompanying an illustration or a photograph.

Diagram – a plan, sketch, drawing or outline designed to demonstrate or explain how something works.

Heading / Headline – a presentational device used to label key information within a text.

Icon – a small image, representing something.

Illustration – something visual such as a drawing, painting or photograph.

Logo – an emblem or icon used to represent a company or organisation.

Subheading – used to break up the text and guide the reader through various sections.

Text box – a box which contains text.

✓ Maximise Your Marks

Being able to differentiate between language features and presentational devices is vital. You will be familiar with a lot of linguistic techniques from your own writing. However, identifying the techniques correctly is important and being able to explain the effect of these techniques is where you will gain marks. Some questions ask you to comment on language or presentational devices. Others might ask you to consider both. In that case, you need to be able to explain how the two things support one another – for example, a picture is generally used to reinforce what has been written.

❓ Test Yourself

1. Rewrite the paragraph below using formal language.

> So I said to the bloke from the garage, 'Oi mate, that banger you flogged me the other day is pants!'
>
> He just shrugged his shoulders and said, 'And?' I was totally miffed!

2. Rewrite the paragraph below using informal language.

> I proceeded to the dining room to eat my supper. 'Good evening,' I said to my mother as we sat down at the table. 'Please could you pass me the water?'

⭐ Stretch Yourself

1. This revision guide is a non-fiction text. Look back over the last few pages and make a note of where the following presentational and linguistic features have been used and why they have been used:
   a) Bullet points
   b) Bold font
   c) Heading
   d) Imperative
   e) Illustration
   f) Diagram
   g) Icon
   h) Alliteration
   i) Rhetorical question

Writing Techniques

Effects of Linguistic Techniques

In addition to being able to identify language features, you will need to be able to explain the effect of the linguistic technique. If you can make more than one point about the technique used you will get a much higher mark.

For example, if a newspaper report used a headline such as 'STRIKER GIVEN THE BOOT' about a player who was recently sacked, you may comment on the effect of this in your exam or controlled assessment:

> The newspaper headline can be read in more than one way. The pun could either be referring to the fact that the player has recently been dismissed or it could be implying that they were literally given a boot. The effect of this is that it is both serious and humorous. It makes the text memorable.

When reading a non-fiction text you also need to explain the impact and effect of non-language features. You need to consider what messages the visual elements of the texts are conveying. The layout is important, and you should remember to consider the effect of other presentational features, such as illustrations and diagrams.

Build Your Understanding

The language techniques that you look at will vary depending on the type of text.

- In texts that are attempting to convince you of something, the language will often be rhetorical, using techniques often used by speakers such as politicians and campaigners. Examples are rhetorical questions, repetition and lists of three.
- In texts that want to engage readers and get them to empathise with the text, pronouns (such as 'you' and 'we') and direct address are used to make you feel as if you are part of the text and believe that it has been written just for you. Anecdotes are used to offer personal experiences to entertain the reader and share similar experiences.
- In texts that are entertaining or descriptive, imagery is often used to help the reader visualise what the writer is saying. Metaphors, similes and personification are all types of imagery and can be very effective in 'painting pictures' for readers (see page 37).
- In informative and explanatory texts, quotations from expert sources and statistics are often used to make the texts seem more believable and reliable. People's opinions are often included and presented in a way that makes them sound factual.

✓ Maximise Your Marks

Always ask 'why?' Why has the writer chosen to use that particular word / phrase / technique? What effect does it have on you as the reader? This will allow you to comment in much more detail and offer an interpretation of the language.

Fact and Opinion

When presented with a variety of non-fiction texts, you will notice that the writers of these texts often use a combination of fact and opinion to get their message across. When you are in the exam you may be asked to distinguish between the two and comment on how writers use fact and opinion:

- A **fact** is something that can be proven to be true – look for statistics and percentages.
- An **opinion** is what somebody thinks. You might notice phrases such as 'in my view' or 'many people think'. The use of emotive or subjective language might indicate that the writer is expressing his or her views, as can the use of modal verbs such as 'should' and 'might'.

Once you have correctly distinguished between the two you then need to be able to explain why the writer has used them. Facts are often used to make the texts more believable and to reinforce the writer's ideas. Opinions can be used to show a variety of people's responses but also to express emotion and beliefs. In some non-fiction texts, writers try to present their opinions as facts to make what they're saying more believable.
Be careful that you acknowledge these examples as opinion and not fact!

Here are some examples of facts and opinions:

FACT

Statistics collected by UNESCO show that there has been very little improvement in literacy in the region.

Her full name is Mary Elizabeth O'Shaughnessy; she used to live next door to us in Doncaster.

Ben Nevis is the highest mountain in the British Isles.

OPINION

It is an absolute disgrace that so few people there can read and write.

Mary Elizabeth was the prettiest girl in the whole of Doncaster.

Many people believe that Ben Nevis presents a relatively easy challenge for the experienced climber.

? Test Yourself

1. Decide which of the examples below are facts and which are opinions.
   a) According to the latest survey, more and more families are buying household items such as televisions and games consoles on credit.
   b) Chris Ashton is the best thing to happen to English rugby since Jonny Wilkinson.
   c) Smoking increases your chance of heart disease by up to 80 per cent.
   d) Governments must invest more in our transport system if we are going to be ready for the 2012 Olympic Games.
   e) Nine out of ten students answered the fact and opinion questions successfully.

★ Stretch Yourself

1. In the following extract identify examples of:
   a) a list of three
   b) repetition
   c) rhetorical question
   d) direct address
   e) metaphor

   > I am appealing to you, as fellow citizens, to help me to end this now. We are drowning in a sea of rubbish. Are you walking around with your eyes shut? Throughout this town there are unemptied bins, vandalised bus shelters and rat infested alleys. We need to take action. Please, fellow citizens, help to end this scandal now.

Audience

Appealing to a Target Audience

It is vital to consider the target **audience** of a text because once you have worked out who the text is aimed at it helps you to read the text more effectively and understand why the writer has made certain choices. Advertisers, in particular, have a clear target audience for their product and adverts are designed specifically to appeal to this target audience.

There are lots of different ways of categorising audiences: through their gender, age, class, hobbies, occupation, etc. Grouping people together like this allows the writers of non-fiction texts to be biased towards that group in order to influence or persuade them. However, this can result in stereotypical representations – it is important to be aware of this when looking at texts because not everybody will adhere to stereotypical ideas. For example, advertisers of cleaning products usually aim their adverts at females because stereotypically it is females who do the 'domestic' chores. However, this is not necessarily accurate and, more recently, advertisers have begun to use males in television commercials for cleaning products too; therefore going against the stereotypical representation of the female as a 'domestic goddess'.

Types of Newspapers

A good example of how texts can differ depending on audience is newspaper writing. There are two main types of national newspaper – broadsheets and tabloids.

- **Broadsheets** – in the past these newspapers such as *The Times* or *The Independent* were generally larger in size. They report national and international news and offer detailed reports of events ranging from politics to finance, current affairs to sporting events. The vocabulary and sentence structure used in broadsheets are also quite sophisticated.
- **Tabloids** – these newspapers are traditionally smaller than broadsheets and often have red mastheads; hence the name 'redtops'. They often include less serious stories and sensationalise the news. These papers feature lots of celebrity stories and often have lots of pictures. The articles themselves tend to be written in a simple and concise way and the story headings often contain features such as puns and alliteration to amuse and entertain the reader.

Both tabloids and broadsheets might run the same newspaper story on their front page. However, they are aimed at different audiences and so the way that the information is delivered varies accordingly. Writers of non-fiction texts always keep their audience in mind – it is fairly unlikely that you would find your younger brother or sister reading *The Times* newspaper!

Understanding the major differences between the two main types of newspaper is important and being able to comment on their layout using the correct terminology will also help you to gain marks. In the writing section of the exam, you might be asked to write a newspaper article and so understanding how an article is put together will also help with your writing skills.

Newspaper Features

Most newspaper front pages include the following features:

- Masthead – the title block of the newspaper.
- Web address – advertises online content.
- Date line – date of publication.
- Slogan – reinforces the identity of the paper.
- Enticement – promotion to help boost newspaper sales.
- Headline – main story details usually in bold.
- Strapline – a subheading that accompanies the main headline.
- Byline – names the reporter who wrote the article.
- Lead story – the main story on the front page.
- Caption – usually underneath a picture to help the reader interpret the images.
- Central image – main picture on a page.
- Standfirst – the introductory paragraph often in bold to grab the reader.

✔ Maximise Your Marks

Most newspapers also have an online version, and although these are examples of web pages, they still include the key features of paper versions. Online newspapers are now a competitive area of the media and give people instant access to the news because they can be updated regularly. Try looking up online versions of newspapers and familiarise yourself with their layout. Think about what is similar to and what is different from the newspaper version.

Masthead — **The Daily News** — Enticement (FREE CD OFFER)

Slogan — Bringing you the news that matters

Date line — 30th September 2011 — www.thedailynews.co.uk — Web address

Lead story — YOUR 20 PAGE GUIDE TO THE WEEK AHEAD — Headline (BRITISH JOURNALIST)

Central image — RELEASED

Caption — Alan Jones released after two years — Strapline

Standfirst — Film star to visit city

by Sarah Smith — Byline

❓ Test Yourself

1. Are the following features more likely to be found in a broadsheet or a tabloid newspaper?
   a) Analysis of foreign news
   b) Articles about celebrities' diets
   c) Pictures that take up most of the front page
   d) Letters to the editor from well-known people
   e) Horoscopes

⭐ Stretch Yourself

1. Find an example of a non-fiction text. Who do you think is the intended audience of the text and why? Pick out key features from the text, presentational devices and linguistic techniques and explain how they are used to appeal specifically to the intended audience.

Writing Non-Fiction

Writing a Non-Fiction Text

Non-fiction writing offers you the chance to write in a variety of different forms, for different purposes and audiences. This means that you could be asked to write an argumentative piece, a persuasive text, a review, or an informative account. It could be an autobiographical extract, a magazine article or a speech for a school assembly.

The pages that follow will look at some of these text types in much more detail and will explain how you craft a piece of writing in that particular style.

Before you start any piece of writing, whether in the exam or for controlled assessment, you must be clear about what it is you are being asked to do. You can also ensure that you are fully prepared by planning your response. For controlled assessment, you are allowed to have notes with you to help with your response. In an exam, taking a few minutes to think about what it is you are going to write can be invaluable – it means that you have a clear structure and will not repeat yourself or waffle on!

Build Your Understanding

With any piece of writing there are a few simple steps that you should take:

1 = Question
2 = Planning
3 = Composing
4 = Checking

The first place to start is with the question that you have been asked – highlight key words so that you know exactly what it is you are being asked to do. Make sure that you know how many marks a question is worth – some non-fiction responses will require you to complete a short and long task. Divide your time according to the marks at stake and make sure that you answer the question. Many people lose marks because they go off topic and write about things that are not related to the question that they have been asked.

Secondly, you should plan! Make a list or mind-map of all the things that you want to include.

There is no right or wrong way of planning – we all have our own individual way of doing things. However, you should not spend too long on your plan. Have a selection of points, key words or stylistic conventions that you know you want to cover and then get on with the writing.

Now that you have worked out what it is you are going to say, you need to get your ideas on to paper and start composing. If you are writing in the exam, the pressure of the 'ticking clock' can cause you to make careless errors. Keep thinking about the basic rules of writing:

- Is it suitable for the intended audience?
- Is it written in paragraphs?
- Is it structured / set out appropriately?
- Does it use a range of punctuation?
- What types of language have you used?
- Have you included linguistic techniques, such as imagery or rhetorical devices?

As well as thinking about the content of your writing, it is also worth thinking about the layout of the piece. If you have been asked to write a magazine article, for example, have you thought about having a catchy heading? You can also include typographic conventions e.g. bullet points, capitalisation or even underlining to draw attention to important elements. You should not write in columns or include drawings or illustrations, though.

Finally, once you have finished writing your response, read it through. Allow yourself time to check your work for errors. You can also go back to your plan and use it as a tick list – checking that you have included everything that you wanted to within your answer.

✓ Maximise Your Marks

As with any piece of writing, it is vital that you make an impact on the reader. Paying attention to the opening and closing paragraphs is important – it allows you to make an impressive first and final impression. The secret to a successful response is to stick to the structure that you planned; use 'discourse markers' and linking phrases to make your writing move fluently and logically from one point to the next; maintain an appropriate tone; avoid waffle; and round up your writing up with a strong conclusion. Do not be afraid to use humour or emotive language: top candidates display a strong personal voice.

Non-Fiction

? Test Yourself

1. What would you say would be your main purpose when writing the following?
   a) A leaflet about how to deal with teenage anxieties.
   b) A speech to a school assembly asking for support for a charity.
   c) A letter to the local newspaper disagreeing with an article you have read.
   d) A step-by-step guide to building a model battleship.
   e) A short story about a funny experience you have had.

★ Stretch Yourself

1. Do a brief plan, using whatever method you prefer, for a response to the following task:

   You have recently returned from a school trip and have been asked to write an article for the school magazine about it.

Writing for Different Audiences

Keeping Your Audience in Mind

In any piece of writing it is important that you know who your intended **audience** is. Before you even begin to put pen to paper, you should consider who is going to read your text and how you can shape and craft it to appeal to them.

Your target audience can vary in **age**, **gender** and **interests** so all these factors need to be considered.

Sometimes you will be writing for an audience of one, for example your Member of Parliament or your best friend; you could be asked to write for quite a narrow audience, perhaps children of a certain age or people who have an interest in a particular subject. Alternatively, you might need to write for a wide audience range, for example if you had to write a speech for a school assembly you would have to appeal to

fellow students and teachers. You may also be writing for a universal audience, in which case your writing would need to have general appeal.

Letters

If you are asked to write a letter then you must open and close it appropriately. For example, if you are addressing someone whose name you do not know, perhaps starting with 'Dear Sir', you should use 'Yours faithfully' to sign off. If you know the person's name and start with 'Dear Mr Brown', for example, you should end your letter with 'Yours sincerely'. Make sure that you spell these correctly: words like 'sincerely' often catch people out!

> 2 Barton Road
> Slingsby
> Brampton
> Lancs
> BS 2 ISR
>
> 7 May 2012
>
> West Land Holidays
> Atlantic Crescent
> Sunnington-on-Sea
> Cumbria
> CB5 7UR
>
> Dear Sir
>
> I am writing to enquire if you have a holiday flat available for early September, this year. The dates I require are as follows: Arrive on Saturday 3 September; Depart Saturday 10 September.
>
> The accommodation would need to sleep four adults and two children (ages eight and ten) and we would need three bedrooms.
>
> I would be grateful if you would let me know if you have suitable accommodation available so that I can make a firm booking.
>
> Thank you.
>
> Yours faithfully
>
> *Heather Brown*
>
> Heather Brown

💡 Boost Your Memory

Remember that:
- Yours faithfully = You do not know the name.
- Yours sincerely = You do know the name.

Build Your Understanding

There are some simple rules that you can follow when writing for specific audiences:

- **Universal audience** – Standard English is essential when you are writing for a universal audience. Make sure that what you write is engaging and that it uses a variety of sentences for effect, has varied vocabulary and follows the standard rules of grammar and punctuation. You should also avoid using vocabulary that is too specialised or expressions that would not be understood by people of all ages.
- **Adults** – if your writing is for adults you can use more sophisticated and complex vocabulary that demonstrates your maturity. You can talk about more sensitive issues, but again you must ensure that you use Standard English throughout. You should try to maintain a formal tone.
- **Young people** – if you are writing for people of your own age, you can use a more colloquial tone. You still have to use Standard English but you may also be able to use text language and slang for effect.
- **Children** – if you are writing for a very young audience it is important that you keep your writing simple but also entertaining. You can do this in non-fiction by thinking about the presentation as well as the language that you use. Children will probably be put off by large chunks of text, so using bullet points and small paragraphs will make it more accessible for them.

✓ Maximise Your Marks

Appealing to your audience means that you consciously think about the language choices that you make. You will be awarded marks for the quality of your sentences and vocabulary, so you need to ensure that these are varied and interesting. You should use a range of simple, compound and complex sentences. Your vocabulary should be varied and appropriate – but do not assume that longer words are always better. You also need to show that you can spell more complex or unusual words correctly.

Register

Register is the language and tone of your writing. The vocabulary and grammar that you use needs to be appropriate for your intended audience.

You alter the register that you use when you are speaking to different people. For example, if you were having a conversation with a teacher about an incident in the playground it would probably be very different from the conversation you would have with your friends about the same incident. The same should be applied to your writing.

When you are given a task, you will need to make choices about the language you use. Most responses will require you to use Standard English. However, there will be occasions when your register will need to be more colloquial.

? Test Yourself

Below are four examples of openings and closings to letters. Which is appropriate for each of the following?

1. A letter to a close friend.
2. A letter to the editor of a newspaper.
3. A letter to your headteacher.
4. A letter to someone whose name you do not know, applying for a job.

a) Dear Katie...Lots of love.
b) Dear Sir...Yours faithfully.
c) Dear Editor...Yours faithfully.
d) Dear Mrs Arbuckle...Yours sincerely.

★ Stretch Yourself

1. Write a brief sentence explaining when and why you might use each of the following in your writing:
   a) Colloquial language
   b) Slang
   c) Standard English
   d) Local dialect
   e) Technical language

Writing to Argue

Writing to Argue

If you are asked to create a piece of **argumentative** writing you will be expected to write a response that includes two **opposing points of view**. You will be arguing either for or against something and to do this successfully you have to acknowledge the opposite point of view. However, it is important that you know which side you are on – and make this absolutely clear to your audience.

The formats you might be asked to write in include:
- letters to newspapers
- blogs
- articles for newspapers or magazines
- letters to Members of Parliament, councillors, school governors, etc.
- speeches, perhaps to fellow students or to a group of adults.

It is often easier to write an argumentative piece if you know something about the subject and feel strongly about it. It can, however, be interesting and challenging to try to put forward a point of view which you do not share.

Build Your Understanding

Argumentative writing should be well structured and organised. To make your argument convincing you need to prove your point. Try using the following techniques:
- Powerful opening – grab the attention of your audience immediately – make your point clear from the outset.
- Use the present tense – it makes your argument contemporary.
- Offer a number of views and opinions, both for and against the subject.
- Ensure that your points are well structured in a logical order.
- Use discourse markers to make your argument flow well.
- Make sure that the language you use is appropriate to the audience – most rhetoric is formal.
- Use rhetorical questions to involve the audience and highlight key thoughts.
- Repetition is an effective way of reinforcing an important point.
- Hyperbole – exaggerate the points that you make to capture your reader's attention.
- Personal pronouns will help make your argument more believable and involve your audience in what you are saying.
- Use counter argument. In other words, give a view you disagree with and say why you think it is wrong.
- Be anecdotal – give specific examples of situations.
- Use a variety of sentence structures.
- Back up the points that you make with evidence.
- Finish with a neat conclusion that reiterates your main points, making your opinion clear.

✓ Maximise Your Marks

To gain a higher grade, you will need to express your opinion clearly and be aware that not everybody will agree with you. When acknowledging the other side of the argument you will need to question that viewpoint and justify the credibility of your reasons. It is also vital that you engage your reader. Word play, humour and other rhetorical devices will make your writing more memorable.

Non-Fiction

Example Response

Look at the example below of a typical argumentative question.

Write an argument supporting the view that homework should be abolished.

Below is an example of a response which uses a range of writing techniques and a variety of sentence structures.

Linking phrases Emotive language

Formal language Opinion as fact

Personal pronouns Hyperbole

Rhetorical questions Counter argument

Good morning staff and fellow students.

I am here today to bring to your attention an issue that I believe is seriously hindering the health of students in school: homework. It is a time-consuming task for both pupils and teachers that I believe is totally unnecessary.

The most important aspect of learning takes place in the classroom – not in your bedroom, study or even at the back of the bus.

Research shows that the average school child spends a third of his or her day in school. The second third is spent sleeping and, if teachers continue to set laborious homework tasks, then the remaining third will be spent working too. When are we young people expected to let off steam? Socialise with our friends and family? Partake in our hobbies? There simply aren't enough hours in the day. The easiest way to give us the time for all this is to abolish homework.

Now, I know that many people will fervently disagree: most teachers believe that homework is an important task that consolidates learning from the classroom. However, research shows that 50 per cent of students copy their homework from a friend. Clearly, this is not strengthening their brainpower; in fact it is probably damaging their friendships and undermining the moral values and ethics of education!

Homework is also problematic for parents. I am sure that we have all been in a situation where we have asked our parents for help with an algebra question only to be met with blank faces. This is embarrassing for the parents and also for students when they have to explain to their tired, grumpy and over worked teacher that they were unable to do their homework because even their parents didn't understand the question.

Consequently, I am proposing that the school council put forward a motion which gives both staff and students the chance to vote anonymously on this matter. I believe that it is our right as young people to live a balanced and happy life – where work and play are combined to make life more pleasurable for everyone.

❓ Test Yourself

❶ Imagine that you have been asked to write an article for your school newspaper arguing that school uniform is a good idea. Try to come up with ideas that counter the points made below:
- Uniform is expensive
- Uniform is uncomfortable
- Uniform is old fashioned
- Uniform prevents your freedom of expression

⭐ Stretch Yourself

❶ Write an argument either supporting or opposing the view that skateboarding should be banned in town and city centres.

Writing to Persuade

Non-Fiction

Writing to Persuade

Writing to **persuade** is very similar to writing to argue – you are trying to convince your audience that your way of thinking is the right way. However, unlike argumentative writing, you only have to acknowledge the side that you believe in. You must ensure that you write appropriately for your audience, have developed points that are fluent and assertive and use a range of rhetorical techniques. Think about the required format for your text as well as the target audience – how will these affect what you write?

The formats you might be asked to write in include:
- letters to politicians, companies or shops
- less formal letters to friends or acquaintances
- leaflets, flyers or posters
- articles for magazines, newspapers or websites
- speeches to various audiences.

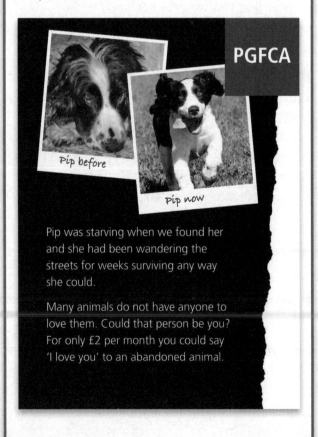

PGFCA

Pip before

Pip now

Pip was starving when we found her and she had been wandering the streets for weeks surviving any way she could.

Many animals do not have anyone to love them. Could that person be you? For only £2 per month you could say 'I love you' to an abandoned animal.

Build Your Understanding

Many of the techniques that you need to include in your persuasive writing are similar to those used when writing to argue. For example:
- Powerful opening – grab the attention of your audience immediately – make your point clear from the outset.
- Use the present tense – this will make your points seem more immediate and relevant.
- Ensure that your points are well structured in a logical order – start with the most relevant issue that adds the most weight to your writing.
- Use discourse markers to make your writing flow well.
- Make sure that the language you use is appropriate to the audience – most rhetoric is formal.
- Use rhetorical questions to involve the audience and highlight key thoughts.
- Repetition and 'lists of three' are effective ways of reinforcing important points.
- Hyperbole – exaggerating the points that you make to capture your reader's attention is particularly relevant in persuasive writing as you want your audience to come round to your way of thinking.
- Personal pronouns will involve your audience and make them feel part of your writing.
- Emotive language – highlighting crucial points in an emotive way will make your audience remember your key points. Emotive language can be sympathetic and humorous – use positive and negative vocabulary to influence your audience.
- Use conditional sentences that make suggestions about what will happen if your audience does not agree.
- Use facts to give your argument weight and even present your opinions in a factual way that makes your writing sound assertive.
- Finish with a neat conclusion that reiterates your main points.

Useful Phrases

To help you get started, here are some useful phrases:

- Some people believe…
- However, the truth of the matter is…
- Do you really think that…
- In my experience…
- What would the consequences be…
- Common sense dictates that…
- All reasonable people think…
- By far the best solution would be…
- Do we really want to…
- It is a terrifying thought that…
- We need to make sure…
- I have no doubt at all that…
- Imagine what would happen if…
- I am sure you will agree that…
- There can therefore be only one conclusion…

✓ Maximise Your Marks

Proofread your writing, check for spelling and grammatical errors. Many students do not leave enough time to read their work back and careless errors lose vital marks. To gain an A or A*, you have to maintain your voice throughout your writing – it is just as important to have a powerful ending as it is to have a powerful opening. Show the examiner that your writing is confident and sustained.

⚲ Boost Your Memory

Use the mnemonic **A FOREST** to help structure a response to the exam question:

A	Anecdotes	Personal stories or experiences to reinforce your point.
F	Facts	Statistics to make your writing more believable – make them up if you do not know any!
O	Opinion	Strong words 'It is outrageous that…'
R	Rhetorical questions	Get your audience thinking – do not forget the question mark!
E	Examples and experts	Give examples as support. Invent an expert and quote him/her.
S	Short, snappy sentences	Make your writing direct and to the point.
T	Triplets	Lists of three will make your key points memorable.

❓ Test Yourself

1. Rewrite the following sentences using Standard English grammar:
   a) We got called into the office even though we never done nothing wrong.
   b) You was well the best.
   c) I would of passed but we got given a dead hard question.
   d) Me and Lee seen Jodie in the precinct.
   e) Give them books to Jo and I.
   f) Me and my mates went to town.
   g) Where's the shops?

★ Stretch Yourself

1. Take five minutes to plan (in whatever form you prefer) an answer to each of the following questions. Then decide which answer you would choose to write.
   a) Your school council has been asked to debate the issue of study leave. Prepare a speech in which you try to persuade the council that study leave should be abolished.
   b) Your school council has been asked to debate the issue of study leave. Write a speech in which you try to persuade the council that study leave is a good thing and should be retained.

Writing to Inform and Explain

Informing and Explaining

Before attempting to answer an informative or explanatory question it is important to understand that, although they share similarities, they too require you to demonstrate different skills.

Informative writing is often factual and requires you to present information clearly and effectively.

Explanatory writing wants you to present your information factually, but it also requires you to explain how and why.

Whereas writing to argue and persuade often results in texts that have an element of bias, writing to inform and explain is more balanced. Information and explanations need to be organised and clear. They also need to be written in a suitable manner and tone.

If you are writing a response in either of these styles of writing then make sure that you choose a topic that interests you or something that you have access to information about. You will also need to ensure that you use examples and explain their effect and purpose – draw comparisons with things that your audience will be able to relate with in order to clarify the points that you make.

✓ Maximise Your Marks

Make sure that your response is well organised and that you use a range of connective phrases to link your ideas. This style of writing provides a good opportunity for using advanced punctuation: you can use a colon to introduce your list of reasons.

Writing to Inform

You should consider the following when writing to inform:

- Your writing needs to be carefully structured in terms of a fluent and logical development, for example: punchy beginning; exploratory and engaging middle; and memorable, hard-hitting end.
- There needs to be a clear sense of progression in your writing.
- You should think carefully about the inclusion of facts and statistics but ensure that these do not take over at the expense of personal views. Try to ensure that you get the balance right.
- If you are using technical language, you might want to offer brief explanations.
- Consider incorporating experts' views (adding weight and gravity to your writing) balanced with your own personal opinion.
- Think carefully about the tone you adopt and choice of language.
- Have a clear view of what you want your writing to achieve.

- You must envisage your intended readership/audience.
- What methods will you employ to get the message/idea across? For example, will you offer real or invented 'scenarios' in your writing to help your reader/audience 'visualise' your point?

BATTLE of the Bands

The event is now in its 10th year and features new talent from the local area

It will take place at the Town Hall on Friday 29th July at 9pm

Tickets cost £5 and are available from the Town Hall Box Office

Writing to Explain

Explanatory writing attempts to explain how and why – it looks at the processes involved in actions, events and behaviours. Writing to explain requires you to break a topic down so that the readers can understand the information more easily. Like the other types of non-fiction writing there are certain features that you should include when writing your response:

- Start with an introductory statement to introduce the topic that you are about to explain. Explanatory writing is usually written in the present tense in chronological order.
- Make sure that you give a range of appropriate detail and specific examples to support your explanations.
- Use connective phrases to link your ideas.
- You could use arrows or shapes to guide your reader through the different sections of your article.

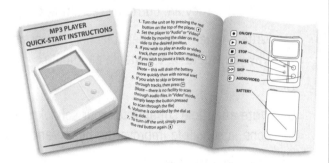

Useful Phrases

To help you get started, look at the examples of sentence starters below.

Writing to inform:
- There are a variety of...
- However, the one that interests me most is...
- By far the most interesting aspect...
- I bet that you didn't know that...
- If you want to...then you need to...
- In order to begin you need to...
- Make sure that you...
- Some people enjoy...
- For more information...

Writing to explain:
- Lots of people want to know how/why...
- Let me explain...
- A good place to start is...
- Another reason...
- The most important...
- Above all else...
- The first thing to do is...
- Contrary to popular belief...
- As a result...
- Consequently...
- Inevitably...

? Test Yourself

1. Rearrange these sentences so that they are in chronological order:
   a) Finally, decorate with crystallised fruit.
   b) Make sure you have all your ingredients ready.
   c) Add the eggs, mixing carefully.
   d) Put into the oven and leave for two hours.
   e) Mix all your dry ingredients.
   f) Ice the cake, using either ready-made icing or icing you have made yourself.
   g) When the eggs have been thoroughly mixed, fold in the dried fruit.

★ Stretch Yourself

1. Choose a subject you already know quite a lot about, for example a hobby or a sport you enjoy, and use the following writing frame to write a short informative/explanatory article, intended for people who know nothing about your subject.

   Lots of people want to know more about...

Practice Questions

 Complete these exam-style questions to test your understanding. Check your answers on pages 89–90. You will need to answer these questions on a separate piece of paper.

Non-Fiction

① Answer **one** question in this section.

You are advised to spend about 25 minutes on the question.

Either

a) Over the summer holidays your school is going to be running a play scheme for younger students. They are currently recruiting people to help out.

Write a letter to your headteacher, **expressing your interest** and **informing** him / her of why you would be a suitable candidate. (30)

Or

b) Write an article suitable for your school newspaper in which you **argue** that more should be done in school to improve the health and fitness of pupils.

You might write about:
- Sports facilities
- The timetable
- School meals
- Health education
- Cycling training (30)

② Answer **one** question in this section.

You are advised to spend about 25 minutes on the question.

Either

a) You have a friend who lives abroad and has never visited your home town or city.

Write a letter to him or her, persuading him/her to stay with you during the summer holidays by describing what your home has to offer a person of your age. (30)

Or

b) Write a speech to be given to the school governors in which you argue either for or against having a school uniform. (30)

3 Answer **one** question. You are advised to spend about 45 minutes on the question.
Your answer will be marked for writing. Plan your answer and write it carefully.
Leave enough time to check it carefully.

Either

a) You have been asked to give a talk to your class about mobile phones, 'a blessing or a curse'. Explain the pros and cons of owning a mobile phone.

You should include:
- The advantages of mobile phone technology.
- The disadvantages of mobile phone technology. (30)

Or

b) Your school is holding a 'charity' day where the normal timetable will be suspended and there will be a range of activities that will make money for the chosen charity. Your headteacher / principal has asked for suggestions about charities to support and ideas for activities.
Write a letter to your headteacher / principal with your suggestions and ideas.

You might write about:
- The background of your chosen charity (this can be fictional) and a brief overview of what it does.
- Why you think it should be supported.
- Details of the activities that you would plan. (30)

4 Answer **one** question. You are advised to spend about 45 minutes on the question.

Your answer will be marked for writing. Plan your answer and write it carefully. Leave enough time to check it carefully.

Either

a) You have been asked to write an article for a teenage magazine on the subject of Saturday jobs for school pupils.

You should include:
- Arguments in favour of young people working while still at school.
- Arguments against young people working while still at school. (30)

Or

b) You have won a competition in a local newspaper and the prize is a three-week trip to a foreign country of your choice. However, the trip must be taken during the school term. Write a letter to your headteacher persuading him or her to authorise your absence.

You might write about:
- What you did to win the prize.
- Where you intend to go and why.
- The potential benefits of the trip both for you and the school. (30)

How well did you do for each question?

| 0–11 | Try again | 12–17 | Getting there | 18–23 | Good work | 24–30 | Excellent! |

Practice Questions

 Complete these exam-style questions to test your understanding. Check your answers on page 90. You may wish to answer these questions on a separate piece of paper.

DAILY WAVE

www.dailywave.co.uk   75p

 **The Waterland**

FREE ADMISSION
FOR PARENTS AND CHILDREN WITH THE DAILY WAVE
Turn to page 4 for more details

EXCLUSIVE! Student Protests Cause Chaos

WE DON'T NEED NO EDUCATION...

Yesterday afternoon thousands of students gathered outside the Conservative Party's headquarters in London in protests against the abolition of EMA and a dramatic rise in university fees.

JUST THE BEGINNING

The NUS estimated that there had been over 50 000 students in the nation's capital and within an hour of being there police arrested 35 people as tension mounted.

Police in riot gear clashed with the protesters, who are angry about the Government's austere measures. Protesters climbed onto the roofs of buildings, smashed windows and started fires to show their growing anger.

The violent approach shocked and astounded many; the NUS distanced themselves from the protest with the President vehemently condemning the vicious scenes.

An angry protestor leaves his mark

Many people had understood and empathised with the students' anger, however, as the rally took a brutal turn and people were injured many people felt that the protesters took their fury too far.

The scale of the protests had exceeded earlier expectations with almost three times as many protesters attending. Originally the ratio of police to protesters had been around 1:90 but with the increased turnout this became more like 1:200.

The march has been the biggest student protest in generations. Students from all over the country gathered to show their fury with the Coalition Government's plans.

With nothing as yet resolved, Metropolitan Police and NUS members confirmed that this is only the beginning.

Full story page 7

The page opposite shows a newspaper's front page. Using this as a stimulus, answer the following four questions.

1 What is the main purpose of the article?

(2)

2 Select two facts from the article.

(2)

3 How does the newspaper's front page use presentational devices to attract the reader's attention?

(8)

4 How does the writer use language to shock and engage the reader?

(8)

(Total: 20)

How well did you do?

| 0–7 | Try again | 8–11 | Getting there | 12–15 | Good work | 16–20 | Excellent! |

Narrative Writing and Genre

Creative Writing Task

Creative writing allows you to show off your imaginative flair, original thinking and descriptive writing techniques. Most exam boards assess creative or imaginative writing through controlled assessment, but you could be asked to write, for example, a short descriptive piece as part of an exam.

The main purposes of creative writing are to **entertain** and **engage** your readers. You will be assessed on your ability to communicate clearly and imaginatively; how well you employ language, style and genre conventions and the technical accuracy of your writing.

The types of tasks that you might be given vary according to your exam board and could include descriptive writing, autobiographical writing, a story, a recreation of a text, even a review of a film or television programme. Each of these tasks is designed to allow you to show off your creative skills.

✔ Maximise Your Marks

Many people enjoy writing creatively. However, it is important to remember that you have not been asked to write a novel – concise, convincing writing will get a much higher mark. The key words for A and A* are 'delight', 'flair' and 'originality'. Your readers must enjoy reading your work and find themselves amused, moved or surprised.

Narrative Writing

Your creative writing task will often – though not always – require you to write a story, whether it is true or fictional. To begin this task you need to think about **plot**, **character** and **theme**.

The plot is made up of the events that take place within a story. Traditionally a story has four parts:
- The introduction or **exposition** in which you introduce your characters, the setting and the circumstance that they find themselves in.
- The **complication(s)** in which you introduce a problem or issue of some sort.
- The **climax**: the high point of the story where the tension reaches its boiling point.
- The **resolution**, where you bring the events of a story to a conclusion.

However, some of the best writing will play around with these four points – introduce some kind of twist or moral, or start at the end and flashback to key events. It is your writing, so it is up to you to make it as original and imaginative as possible.

Genre

The chosen **genre** of a piece of writing is important because it provides the writers with a range of stylistic conventions that they can employ in their writing. There are many different types of genre and a text can include elements of more than one:

- Horror
- Romance
- Mystery
- Gothic
- Fantasy
- War
- Science fiction
- Comedy
- Fairy tale
- Ghost stories
- Action/adventure
- Autobiography

You may be asked to write in a particular genre or you may be free to choose your own. Once you have decided upon a genre for your piece of writing, you then have to consider the stylistic conventions of that particular genre.

This can have an impact on the choice of setting for your writing and the types of character that you will include.

The genre you choose will also influence your style. For example, in a piece of horror writing you would want to create tension and suspense. Consequently, your sentences might be short and sharp, your imagery dark and gruesome and your characters might have a sinister side. Your opening might also set the scene somewhere dark and mysterious, and an ominous atmosphere could be created through something as simple as the weather.

However, it is also interesting in creative writing to experiment with genre conventions. Stephenie Meyer's *Twilight* saga is a good example of this and has been phenomenally successful. Although her vampire main character Edward does share features with the more common vampire stereotypes inspired by Bram Stoker's *Dracula*, elements such as Edward's vegetarian diet show how Stephenie Meyer has altered the stylistic conventions of genre.

Narrative Hooks

How many times have you opened a book, read the first page and then been totally hooked? Creating a powerful opening is essential. Nothing is more important than the beginning; you need to engage your reader from the start. This is done by using narrative hooks – these can be a range of different techniques that immediately create a specific impact and encourage your reader to keep reading:

- The question hook – you want the reader to read on, to find the answer.
- The atmospheric hook – this is descriptive, and could evoke a variety of moods.
- The direct speech hook – this implies lots of action and a fast pace.
- The visual hook – this paints a vivid picture in the mind of the reader and allows them to visualise what is going on.
- The funny hook – this is a tricky hook and works if it appeals to your sense of humour.

? Test Yourself

1 What narrative hooks are the following examples of?
   a) 'Get out of here,' she screamed.
   b) As he left, the moon emerged from behind the cloud and its silver light spread across the lake.
   c) I knew I was in trouble, but what had I done?

★ Stretch Yourself

1 Make a list of ten books or stories you have read (either in school or at home) and, looking at the list of genres above, say which genre you think each belongs to. Remember that writers often draw on more than one genre.

Characterisation and Imagery

Effective Characterisation

Once you have an idea about what is going to happen in your creative piece, you can start thinking about the **characters**.

A character needs to be believable and in order for that to happen you need to think about their physical description, their back story (what has happened to them so far in their life and how their past has had an impact on their present), their personality, their beliefs and their relationships.

In creative writing we portray characters through their actions, their speech and the ways in which people respond to them, as well as through description.

Your choice of verbs and adverbs is important as it provides more information and your readers are able to make inferences about the characters.

Narrative Viewpoint

Another important element of creative writing is deciding from which viewpoint you are going to write your piece.

A **first person narrator** tells the story from within the text and would be the type of perspective you would choose for an autobiography or a character that you are writing as yourself. This type of narrative requires you to use the pronoun 'I', for example: 'I first realised that my family wasn't exactly what you'd call ordinary when I was nine years old.'

First person narrative is very common and some people feel that this is the most natural way to tell a story. However, there are drawbacks. First person narratives only offer a one-dimensional perspective; the reader is solely reliant on the narrator's point of view. One way to overcome this is to use **split narrative**, where you have more than one narrator. This is a technique that, when it is done well, is very effective.

Second person narrative is when you use 'you' for your narrative perspective, for example, 'You might not realise just yet, but the events that will take place today, will change your life forever.' It can be difficult to maintain this perspective throughout your piece of writing.

A **third person narrator** stands outside of the text and is often referred to as an **omniscient narrator**. In third person narrative you refer to the characters using 'he', 'she', 'they' and by name. Third person narrators are usually 'omniscient' or all-knowing and can tell us everything that is going on, delving into their characters' minds.

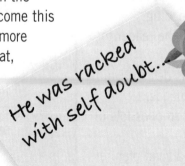

He was racked with self doubt...

Imagery

Creative writing gives you an opportunity to show your expertise at writing: it is a perfect opportunity to take your reader on a journey into your work. In most creative and descriptive writing this is done by using **imagery**.

The literary techniques that come under the imagery umbrella include: **simile**, **metaphor**, **personification**, **symbolism**, **pathetic fallacy** and **sensory description**.

✓ Maximise Your Marks

The examples below are all linked to visual elements of creative writing – painting pictures with your words. However, you can also use word play and language to create interesting sound effects. **Alliteration**, **assonance** and **onomatopoeia** are all techniques that work through sound to create effects in your writing (see page 74). Candidates who gain higher marks will use language artfully and avoid clichéd ideas.

Technique	Definition	Example
Simile	A comparison using the words 'like' or 'as'; a common figure of speech used in writing.	His stomach rumbled like Vesuvius.
Metaphor	A metaphor also compares things. However, it is a direct comparison that does not use 'like' or 'as'.	His sapphire eyes were still blue pools.
Personification	Personification is where inanimate objects are given human qualities.	The first rays of morning tiptoed through the meadow.
Symbolism	Symbolism is used to provide meaning to the writing beyond what is actually being described. Symbols are objects, characters, colours and figures used to represent abstract ideas or concepts.	Where once there had been a bloody battle, I now saw a field of poppies stretching before me.
Pathetic fallacy	Pathetic fallacy refers to how the weather and elements of nature are used to reflect the mood of the characters or the situation.	The cold wind breathed its air on my face, whilst the rain cried on my shoulder.
Sensory description	Sensory description is an important part of imagery that evokes the reader's senses. It describes things that can be heard, seen, smelt, touched and tasted.	As I lay in the summer sun, the smell of charcoal from the barbecue lingered in the air.

? Test Yourself

1 Complete the following examples of simile and metaphor with appropriate comparisons:

   a) The moon glowed like...

   b) Rain fell from the sky like...

   c) Dewdrops glistened on the glass like...

   d) The crows cackled like...

   e) The road wound its way up the mountain like...

   f) The sea was...

   g) Her eyes were...

★ Stretch Yourself

1 Look at the extract below; what impression do you get of the characters and why?

> The classroom door burst open and was now pirouetting on its hinge.
>
> 'Hiiiiyyyyaaa,' the martial arts teacher bellowed as he karate chopped through the air. He scanned the classroom as he fell to his feet.
>
> 'Just another ordinary supply teacher,' whispered James sarcastically as the teacher straightened his karate suit.

Transforming Texts

Recreating a Text

For some creative writing tasks, you will be asked to take an existing text and transform it into another genre. Although this might not seem 'original', the best writers are those who can adapt and transform texts into something new. This type of writing enables you to demonstrate the typical conventions of the form that you choose and also enrich your writing through a new perspective.

The possibilities for this type of writing are rich and varied. You could take a poem and turn it into a dramatic monologue, elaborating the persona's thoughts and feelings. You could turn a piece of travel writing into a website page or an extract from a Shakespeare play into a scene from a soap opera. The important thing to remember is to use the appropriate conventions for your new format and to use subtle changes of tone and vocabulary.

For example, look at how a short scene from William Shakespeare's *Romeo and Juliet* could be turned into the script for a television chat show:

In the original format (Act 3, Scene 5 of *Romeo and Juliet*), Juliet is told that her father has arranged her wedding to the wealthy and eligible bachelor Count Paris. However, her parents do not know that she is already married to Romeo. She argues with her father, who cannot understand why she is unwilling to go through with the wedding. The scene culminates with Lord Capulet threatening to disown his daughter if she continues to defy him.

A new script format for a television chat show, *When Life Gives You Lemons* could begin:

Show host: 'Good morning and welcome to *When Life Gives You Lemons* with me, Nicky White. On today's show we have a family at breaking point – a fourteen year old girl who has gone behind her parents' backs and embarked on a relationship with a boy her parents despise. Today, we're going to help the family turn their lemons into lemonade as we get to the bottom of what's been going on. So, please put your hands together and welcome to the stage, fourteen year old Juliet.'

✓ Maximise Your Marks

To gain a higher grade with this type of task you need to take inspiration from the original – perhaps using its theme, its characters or its setting. You need to be constantly aware of the demands of your new form and your intended audience. It should entertain, move or inspire on its own merits, while giving new insights into the original text.

Build Your Understanding

The quality of what you write will depend not just on your use of stylistic conventions, but on how well you use basic writing tools, such as vocabulary, sentence structure and paragraphing.

Using a thesaurus is a great idea; however, you need to make sure that you do not overdo it. Sometimes saying things in their simplest form is also effective. When you are using common words that can easily be repeated such as 'nice' and 'said' a thesaurus is a great study aid. Finding synonyms for words like 'said' can also help with characterisation. For example, if you wanted to create tension and suspense, your character might 'whisper' or the sound might 'echo'. To ensure your chosen synonym has the precise meaning you want, use a dictionary to check its meaning.

In creative writing, it is important to remember to use a variety of sentence structures. You should think about the rhythm of your writing – long, descriptive sentences can create a feeling of flow and continuity but they can become over-complicated. Similarly, short sentences are excellent for creating impact and drama, but even more effective is a simple, short paragraph.

Just as you are conscious about the ways that you start your sentences, also think about the punctuation that you use at the end. For example, the use of ellipses (…) is an effective way of creating tension and withholding information.

✓ Maximise Your Marks

Once you have an idea for this type of writing, you have to bring that idea to life. Teachers and examiners are looking for control as well as creativity. To achieve a good grade, you should:

- write in the appropriate manner for the genre and purpose of your text
- use a range of sentences and vocabulary to keep the reader's interest
- use literary and linguistic devices such as simile and metaphor to show rather than tell
- develop characters, settings and themes within your narrative
- be consistently accurate with spelling, grammar and punctuation
- show control, flair and originality in your writing.

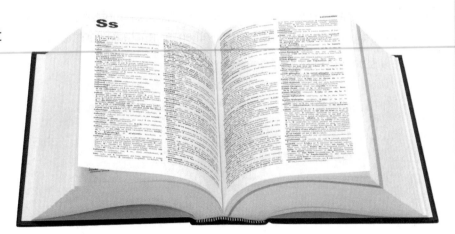

❓ Test Yourself

1. Take a well-known fairy tale such as *The Three Little Pigs* and imagine that you are using the events of the story to inspire a newspaper article. Devise a heading for the article, and try to use an example of alliteration, rhyme or pun in your heading to make it memorable.

★ Stretch Yourself

1. Write the whole of the article described in the Test Yourself section.

Practice Questions

Complete these exam-style questions to test your understanding. Check your answers on page 91. You may wish to answer these questions on a separate piece of paper.

1 You will be assessed on both your ability to produce an interesting, organised and appropriate piece of writing and the use of varied sentence structures and correct spelling, grammar and punctuation.

Write about a childhood memory.

(30)

2 You will be assessed on both your ability to produce an interesting, organised and appropriate piece of writing and the use of varied sentence structures and correct spelling, grammar and punctuation.

Write a story entitled 'The Journey'.

(30)

3 Write an article for a magazine about a time when you faced a challenge in your life.

and then

Write a letter to the magazine from someone who has read your letter and felt inspired by it.

Creative Writing

(30)

4 Choose a character from a novel or short story that you have read in class and write a short series of diary entries about events after the story has finished.

and either

i) Imagine that the diary has been published after the character's death. Write a review of it.

or

ii) Write the script of an interview of the character on a radio show.

(30)

How well did you do for each question?

| 0–11 | Try again | 12–17 | Getting there | 18–23 | Good work | 24–30 | Excellent! |

Studying Shakespeare

William Shakespeare

As part of your GCSE English Literature exam you will have to complete a Shakespeare task. This could be part of a controlled assessment or an exam. You may be asked to analyse a complete Shakespeare play, a short section of a play or both. You will have to look at a range of features such as **character**, **plot**, **themes**, **language** and **context**. You may also have to compare the Shakespeare play that you have studied with another text, or you may be studying a modern version of a Shakespeare play in the form of a film or theatrical production.

Some students are daunted by the thought of studying Shakespeare. However, Shakespeare is still popular for a reason. His themes are still relevant today – love, hate, relationships, family problems.

The Shakespearean plays that you are studying were written to be performed – they are exciting pieces of drama – and it is important that you watch the play that you are studying too.

It does not matter whether you see a film version of the play or a theatre performance; seeing it performed will help bring it to life and deepen your understanding of plot, character, themes and language.

Most of Shakespeare's plays were first performed outside in the daylight and the actors had very little access to props, fancy costumes and scenery. Instead, Shakespeare's language took the audience on an exciting journey into a different world. Another major difference between watching a play then and now is that all of the characters would have been played by males; women were not allowed to act in the theatre.

The Bard of Avon

When studying the work of William Shakespeare it is important to know a little bit about the man who is considered to be the world's greatest playwright. It will help you understand his work if you are able to put the play that you are studying into context. This means that you need to have an awareness of the historical, cultural and literary traditions that underpin his work.

Shakespeare was born in Stratford-upon-Avon into quite a wealthy middle-class family. He went to a grammar school and then married Anne Hathaway. They had three children together, but Shakespeare left his family and travelled to London to work as an actor and playwright. Shakespeare became highly praised quite quickly and ended up partially owning the Globe Theatre in London.

During his career there were two different monarchs on the throne: Elizabeth I (1558–1603) and James I (1603–1625). James became the patron of Shakespeare's theatre company, which was renamed The King's Men in his honour. Shakespeare was popular with people from all sections of society and his plays reflected the interests and concerns of those for whom he wrote.

Although Shakespeare's work is very well known, little is actually known about him. What we do know is that his collection of work is made up of at least 37 plays and 154 sonnets – and it is from this collection of plays and poetry that your GCSE texts will be taken.

Types of Play

The plays of William Shakespeare can be loosely categorised into three different genres – each genre having its own defining features.

Tragedy

Shakespeare's tragedies include *Macbeth*, *Romeo and Juliet*, *Othello*, *Hamlet* and *King Lear*. They usually end with the death of the **protagonists** (main characters), often referred to as the tragic heroes. The deaths of these characters have a huge impact on the people around them and often the larger community too. Death is not just confined to the tragic heroes either – there will be other victims as part of the tragic chain of events. Before they die, the heroes will usually reach a 'peak' in the play – of happiness, fortune or achievement. This is often short-lived and, after this peak, events take a terrible turn for the worse. The heroes are usually responsible in some way for this change in fortune. Most of these characters have some kind of 'flaw' within their personality. This is sometimes referred to as 'hamartia' – or 'the fatal flaw' – and originates from Greek Tragedy. There is usually an element of fate too – this almost makes the tragedy inevitable.

History

Many of Shakespeare's plays, such as *Macbeth* and *Julius Caesar*, have historical elements. However, these plays are more commonly thought of as tragedies. Only ten of Shakespeare's plays are normally referred to as 'histories' and these share common features. They are all set against English Medieval history and attempt to provide some kind of social commentary. Although Shakespeare based them on accounts of real historical events, nowadays they are not thought to be entirely accurate. The 'histories' include *Richard II*, *Henry IV* Parts I and II, *Henry V* and *Richard III*.

Comedy

It is important to remember that in the Shakespearean period 'comedy' had a different meaning from today. A Shakespearean comedy usually has a happy ending, often involving the marriage of characters who have been on an emotional roller coaster during the play. This genre usually includes lots of intertwining plots, themes of betrayal and conflict, often within a family, some broad vulgar comedy from working class characters and a pastoral element – courtly people living an idealised, rural life. Among Shakespeare's best known comedies are *Twelfth Night*, *A Midsummer Night's Dream*, *Much Ado About Nothing* and *As You Like It*.

✓ Maximise Your Marks

To gain high marks, you need to show that you can use appropriate terminology properly. For example, you should refer to the main character in any literary text as the protagonist. You might also refer to some of the **conventions** of the genre you are discussing, such as the fatal flaw in tragedy or the pastoral element in comedy.

❓ Test Yourself

❶ What are the defining features of each of the following genres?

    a) Tragedy
    b) History
    c) Comedy

⭐ Stretch Yourself

❶ Look at the Shakespeare play you have been studying:

    a) Which genre do you think it belongs to?
    b) Which of the typical elements of the genre, described above, does it include?

Shakespeare's Use of Language

Commenting on Language

Shakespeare used different types of language in his plays.

Blank verse

This is verse that is written in **iambic pentameter** – lines which generally have syllables, with every second syllable stressed:

But <u>soft</u>, what <u>light</u> through <u>yonder</u> <u>window</u> <u>breaks</u>?

This verse is used by Shakespeare in a wide range of situations because it sounds similar to the ordinary rhythms of English without being too artificial. Most of Shakespeare's plays, including his characters' most famous speeches, are in blank verse.

Prose

Prose is easy to distinguish from verse because it looks like everyday speech. It does not have a regular rhythm. It is mostly used by comic characters, by characters of low status and by higher status characters when they are exchanging witticisms.

Rhyming couplet

A rhyming couplet is a pair of rhymed lines often used by Shakespeare as a summative device to signal the end of important sections or summarise key thoughts and feelings:

Two such opposed kings encamp them still/ In man as well as herbs – grace and rude will.
(Friar Laurence in *Romeo and Juliet*.)

Shakespearean Imagery

There are many different plays that you could study and the **imagery** that you come across will vary depending on the genre of play that you are studying. However, there are common techniques that you need to be able to identify and explore. Shakespeare uses imagery to elaborate on key points in the dialogue and emphasise key themes and issues. It is worth looking for patterns in the imagery. For example, in *Othello* you will find a lot of animal imagery:

Goats and monkeys!

and in *Romeo and Juliet* a lot of images relate to light and darkness:

It is the east and Juliet is the sun.

Build Your Understanding

Shakespeare was a master of language and, like many other poets and playwrights of his time, liked playing around with language techniques.

He used puns and double entendres regularly to comic effect. For example, Mercutio uses lots of puns in *Romeo and Juliet*:

Tybalt, you rat-catcher...

Romeo and Juliet is also full of oxymorons, which is a technique that uses conflicting ideas or contrasting language joined together, for example *brawling love* and *honourable villain*.

Plot Structure

Shakespeare's plays are made up of **scenes** and **acts**. Shakespeare structured his plays carefully. For example, in a tragedy a comic scene often precedes an important climax, releasing tension before it is built again.

Most of his plays are made up of five acts – the first act is used to introduce you to the main characters and there is often a prologue. The third act usually contains dramatic scenes where elements of the plot reach their dramatic climax. The fifth act is usually used to show that order has been restored and the characters live happily ever after (or not, in the case of tragedies and histories!).

Recurring Themes, Ideas and Messages

A **theme** is the subject matter of a text, perhaps a message or idea, and often there are several themes that run through a Shakespeare play. These vary depending on the genre of the play; however, many themes are evident throughout the work of Shakespeare.

Love, marriage and relationships

Most of Shakespeare's plays examine the theme of love – this could be dutiful love to family and friends or romantic love, both of which are subjects of *Romeo and Juliet*. Marriage is often used in his comedies and is a way of restoring harmony between characters, although the characters encounter many obstacles on the way, often not recognising love until it is almost too late (like Benedick and Beatrice in *Much Ado About Nothing*).

Religion

Religion is important in many of Shakespeare's plays and can be linked to other elements, such as death, ghosts, appearance and reality, and the supernatural. Macbeth rejects God and religion, embracing evil instead. *Romeo and Juliet* uses religious imagery and their union is blessed by the Friar, but some audience members might feel that by defying their parents and, ultimately killing themselves, they too are sinners.

Fate

Fate is a key theme in lots of Shakespeare's work – some of the characters seem to be locked in a hopeless battle against their destiny. There are constant references to fate and 'the stars' in plays such as *King Lear*, *Romeo and Juliet* and *Julius Caesar*.

Nature

Nature is another key theme in all of Shakespeare's plays and can be linked to human nature and also the nature of the society in which we live, whether in pastoral comedies like *As You Like It* or tragedies like *Macbeth*.

Conflict

Conflict is another important theme in many of Shakespeare's plays, particularly the tragedies and historical plays. Many of these chronicle real wars and battles from history (for example *Richard III* and *Antony and Cleopatra*), but the conflict between the characters and their ideas is just as important as what happens on the battlefield.

Power

Power is an important theme in many of Shakespeare's plays. Characters in tragedies, histories and comedies are shown abusing their power, but at the end of the play justice and balance are always restored.

Shakespeare

? Test Yourself

1. Are any of the following language techniques used in the quotations below?
   - an oxymoron
   - a pun
   - a metaphor
   - a simile
   - a rhyming couplet
   a) 'A little more than kin, and less than kind.'
   b) '...oaths are straws; mens faiths are wafer-cakes.'

⭐ Stretch Yourself

1. Look at the Shakespeare play you have been studying and note the ways in which Shakespeare explores the following themes:
   a) Love
   b) Religion
   c) Fate
   d) Nature
   e) Conflict
   f) Power

Romeo and Juliet

Romeo and Juliet

Romeo and Juliet (1597) is probably the most famous of Shakespeare's plays. Since its first performance at the end of the sixteenth century it has constantly been in performance.

The genre of the play is a **romantic tragedy**: the two protagonists fall madly in love despite being from rival families; they defy their family feud and get married in the hope that their young, passionate love will reunite their families.

However, true to its tragic conventions, fate has a different end in store and the lovers lose their lives. Their deaths, however, restore the friendship between their feuding families.

The play has proved to be so popular because the self-destructive passion of the two young lovers is completely at odds with the world in which they live. The idea of forbidden love and careless romance is something that we can all relate to and is often explored in literature, film and theatre.

Build Your Understanding

Demonstrate a wider understanding of literature and Shakespeare by showing that you have read around the subject and can put it in context. Shakespeare took inspiration for *Romeo and Juliet* from a narrative poem written in 1562 by Arthur Brooke called the *Tragical History of Romeus and Juliet*. You might want to explore the differences between Brooke's story and Shakespeare's play.

You can also talk about the play's lasting impact – *Romeo and Juliet* has gone on to inspire many contemporary writers. For example, *West Side Story* is a musical set in 1950s New York and is a modern, musical adaptation of Shakespeare's play. Baz Luhrmann's 1990s version keeps Shakespeare's words but changes the time and place. Think about how these versions re-interpret the story.

💡 Boost Your Memory

To distinguish between the title of the play and the names of the characters, remember to put quotation marks around the title of the play 'Romeo and Juliet'. If you are typing your response you should italicise the title: *Romeo and Juliet*.

✔ Maximise Your Marks

It can be helpful to mention the social and historical context of the play. To gain high marks, make sure any such comments are clearly linked to the text. Do not make vague sweeping statements, such as 'women had no power in those days'. Be more precise, for example: 'a girl of Juliet's class would be expected to accept her father's choice of husband, so it is unsurprising that he reacts violently'. You should also remember that not all members of the audience, then or now, would have the same opinion.

Characters

There is always a hierarchy of **characters** within a Shakespearean play and in *Romeo and Juliet* it looks like this:

- Prince Escalus – he is the Prince of Verona and as the authoritative figure, it is his responsibility to keep public peace.
- Count Paris and Mercutio are kinsmen of the Prince – Count Paris is connected to the Capulets because he wants to marry Juliet, and Mercutio is Romeo Montague's best friend.
- The Capulet household – Capulet is the patriarch of the Capulet household, Lady Capulet is his wife and Juliet is his daughter. Tybalt is Juliet's cousin.
- The Montague household – Montague is the patriarch of the Montague household and is husband to Lady Montague and father to Romeo. Benvolio is Romeo's cousin.
- Friar Laurence is Verona's Catholic 'holyman' and is friend to both Capulet and Montague. The Friar is an important character in terms of plot development and his neutrality is central to the play.
- The nurse has brought Juliet up and has cared for her since she was a baby. She is a comic character who is lower in status than the rest of the Capulets.
- There is then a range of minor characters and also the chorus, who we assume is a group of people, but is in fact an individual character, who functions as a narrator and offers commentary on the play.

Themes

Two of the main **themes** in *Romeo and Juliet* are the contrasting themes of **love** and **hate**. Love is presented in a number of ways from the initial unrequited love between Romeo and Rosaline, to the young passionate love of the two protagonists. Love is also portrayed through family relationships and friendships. This dutiful love creates all kinds of tensions as Juliet is forced to adhere to her father's wishes and marry Paris, which ultimately leads to her death. It is Mercutio's duty and honour to his friend Romeo that leads to his death. Love changes everything in *Romeo and Juliet*. In contrast, hatred is shown through the Capulet/Montague feud, and it is this hatred that creates the conflict.

Another key theme in *Romeo and Juliet* is the idea of **fate** – the prologue refers to Romeo and Juliet as 'star cross'd lovers', suggesting that they were destined to be with each other. The two lovers are fated to be together in life or death – there are lots of references throughout the play to this.

❓ Test Yourself

1. Make a list of the main characters in the Shakespeare play you have been studying and briefly describe their functions.

⭐ Stretch Yourself

1. Identify three of the main themes in the play you have studied and write a brief paragraph on each.

Writing an Essay on *Romeo and Juliet*

Romeo and Juliet, Act 3, Scene 5

When studying Shakespeare you will be asked to write an essay looking at a key element of the play that you have been studying.

To demonstrate how to do this, the following few pages will look at an extract from *Romeo and Juliet*; a sample essay question; and a plan of how to approach an essay.

The scene starts just as day is breaking in Juliet's bedroom. Romeo is preparing to leave for Mantua after being exiled there as punishment for killing Tybalt. Juliet tries to convince her new husband to stay and is overcome with love. Romeo declares that he would be willing to do anything for Juliet, even risk his life by staying if that is what she wants.

Faced with such a prospect, Juliet changes her mind and then the Nurse enters to warn Juliet of her mother's impending arrival. The lovers bid farewell and Juliet is disturbed by the 'pale' appearance of her lover whom she thinks resembles somebody in a tomb.

Lady Capulet arrives and mother and daughter have an ambiguous conversation, at the end of which, Lady Capulet tells her daughter of Capulet's marriage plans for her. Juliet is horrified by the proposal and rejects the match.

Capulet enters and is enraged by his daughter's defiance. He threatens to disown her as Juliet's desperate pleas fall on deaf ears.

The scene ends with Juliet turning to her nurse for help. Upset by her nurse's disloyalty, she hurries to Friar Laurence, so distraught that if he is unable to help, then she sees suicide as her only option.

A possible assignment question might read:

Focusing on Act 3, Scene 5 of *Romeo and Juliet* explore how the theme of love is presented in this scene.

The first thing to do is to make sure that you understand exactly what the question is asking you to do – explore the key theme of love. Explore, means that you have to look at this theme in detail and in order to get a high grade you will need to make references to the play as a whole.

Some exam boards might ask you to show how the theme of love is presented in this scene in the form of a multi-modal presentation; this means that you do not have to write an essay but can produce a response that uses a presentation or a video.

Alternatively, you could be asked to compare how love is presented in this scene and another text – this could be a poem or a filmed adaptation.

Introduction to Your Essay

You need to begin by referring to key words in the question and putting the question into context. You could give a very brief **synopsis** of the play and explain that, despite being a tragedy, love is central to this play. You should use your introduction to give your initial response and explain how you are going to answer the essay question.

Main Body of Your Essay

The main body of your essay needs to be your exploration of the key scene.

- Section one – young passionate love – look at the dialogue that takes place between Romeo and Juliet. What inferences do we make as we see him leave her room? What techniques does Shakespeare use in their language to highlight the young passionate elements of their love?
- Section two – doomed love – what references are there to what fate has in store for our two tragic heroes? Are any recurring motifs or symbols used to highlight their fate? Think about references to light and darkness. How does their meeting end?
- Section three – parental love – what do we learn about Juliet's relationship with her mother at the start of this scene?
  What is the effect of all of the double entendres in their speech? How does the mood change with the arrival of Capulet? What type of parental love is portrayed here? Caring? Tyrannical? What techniques does Shakespeare use to show this side of Capulet?
- Conclusion – your conclusion needs to refer back to the question and sum up the main points of your argument. Why is love so important to the play as a whole? How does love change things? Were Romeo and Juliet right to do as they did?

❓ Test Yourself

1 Society was very religious when Shakespeare wrote and staged this play. Why might some of the ideas contained in it have been controversial?

⭐ Stretch Yourself

1 Make notes about the depiction of religion and attitudes towards religion in the play you have studied.

Writing an Essay on *Romeo and Juliet*

Example Response

Look at the P.E.E. example paragraphs that follow to see how love is explored in this scene – can you find other examples from within this scene to make similar points?

Young passionate love

P In Act 3, Scene 5, the two young lovers are bidding farewell to each other. The audience assumes that the two have consummated their marriage and now it is time for Romeo to leave for Mantua. Juliet is trying to put off what will be a painful farewell.

E *Wilt thou be gone? It is not yet near day.*
It was the nightingale and not the lark
That pierced the fearful hollow of thine ear.

E This section of the scene is important as it depicts Romeo leaving Juliet's chamber. We hear Juliet attempt to persuade Romeo to stay. She wants him to believe that day has not dawned so that they can be together for longer. The verb 'pierced' is effective as it suggests that their harmony has been broken. This could also be a reference to Juliet's virginity, which symbolises the physical aspect of their young passionate love.

Doomed love

P As the doomed lovers say their final goodbyes, Juliet has an 'ill divining soul' and is terrified about when she will next see her husband.

E *Methinks I see thee, now thou art below.*
As one dead in the bottom of a tomb.

E This is one of many premonitions about the death of the protagonists. It links to themes of fate and destiny. Romeo and Juliet can only be together in death. This perfectly exemplifies how their love is doomed. The consequences of falling in love are out of their hands and written in the stars.

Parental love

P One of the important aspects of this scene is the switch that Juliet makes from wife to daughter. In the patriarchal society of Verona, Juliet would be answerable to her father. However, we have just witnessed her deceive her parents by marrying the son of their enemy and spending the night with him in her chamber. The romantic mood of the scene changes to one of anger when her father arrives to ask if her mother has given her the news about her arranged marriage to Count Paris.

E *How now, wife? Have you delivered to her our decree?*

E The question immediately asserts Capulet's authority. The language that he uses here reinforces his authority as her father. The word 'decree' has legal connotations; the plans are now final. In a patriarchal society Juliet, as a woman and daughter, would have to abide by her father's rules and wishes. This element of the scene portrays an aspect of parental love – it is Juliet's duty to do as her father requests.

When analysing a scene from a Shakespeare play it is important to make links and connections to the rest of the play.

You need to demonstrate your understanding of how the scene fits into the play as a whole. Think about the following:

- What happened before this extract to lead to the events shown here.
- How things change during this scene – it is likely that the chosen scene will feature an important plot development.
- How the characters have changed from the beginning of the play.
- The implications of the events that take place in this scene and how what happens influences the rest of the play.
- How the themes depicted in this scene are shown in other parts of the play.
- Whether the language and imagery used here are echoed in other parts of the play.

Comparing Shakespeare to Another Text

Some exam boards will ask you to look at an extract from a Shakespeare play and then compare it to another text. For example, you could be asked to compare how love is presented in Act 3, Scene 5 of *Romeo and Juliet* with love in Carol Ann Duffy's poem *Anne Hathaway*.

There are many links between the two texts as Anne Hathaway was Shakespeare's wife. Duffy's poem is written in Anne's 'voice', reflecting on her relationship with Shakespeare after his death. The poem focuses on the sexual relationship of a married couple. Similarly, in the key scene from *Romeo and Juliet* we are presented with the passionate love of the two protagonists – but they are just starting their relationship, which will be tragically cut short.

? Test Yourself

1. What are the different kinds of love shown in *Romeo and Juliet*?
2. If you have studied a different play, say how many of these different kinds of love are present in the play you have studied.

★ Stretch Yourself

1. To help your understanding of how they relate to each other in terms of the plot and structure, select the key scenes from the play you have studied and make a 'storyboard'.

Practice Questions

 Complete these exam-style questions to test your understanding. Check your answers on pages 91–92. You will need to answer these questions on a separate piece of paper.

1 *Macbeth*

Answer **both** parts of the question. You are advised to spend about 40 minutes on the question.

a) How does Shakespeare show Macbeth's reluctance to kill the King in the extract below?

To answer this question you will need to comment on:
- Language – ideas and meaning.
- Structure – relevance to the rest of the play.
- Character.
- Effect on the audience.
- Social and historical context. (15)

Extract
Act I, Scene vii
Court of Macbeth's castle.

MACBETH
If it were done when 'tis done, then 'twere well
It were done quickly: if the assassination
Could trammel up the consequence, and catch
With his surcease success; that but this blow
Might be the be-all and the end-all here,
But here, upon this bank and shoal of time,
We'd jump the life to come. But in these cases
We still have judgment here; that we but teach
Bloody instructions, which, being taught, return
To plague the inventor: this even-handed justice
Commends the ingredience of our poison'd chalice
To our own lips. He's here in double trust;
First, as I am his kinsman and his subject,
Strong both against the deed; then, as his host,
Who should against his murderer shut the door,
to bear the knife myself. Besides, this Duncan
Hath borne his faculties so meek, hath been
So clear in his great office, that his virtues
Will plead like angels, trumpet-tongued, against
The deep damnation of his taking-off;
And pity, like a naked new-born babe,
Striding the blast, or heaven's cherubin, horsed
Upon the sightless couriers of the air,
Shall blow the horrid deed in every eye,
That tears shall drown the wind. I have no spur
To prick the sides of my intent, but only
Vaulting ambition, which o'erleaps itself
And falls on th'other.
Enter LADY MACBETH.

How now! what news?

and

b) Show how Shakespeare presents Macbeth's character in another part of the play. (15)

2 *Romeo and Juliet*

Answer **both** parts of the question. You are advised to spend about 40 minutes on the question.

a) How does Shakespeare present love in the extract below?

To answer this question you will need to comment on:
- Language – ideas and meaning.
- Structure – relevance to the rest of the play.
- Character.
- Effect on the audience.
- Social and historical context.   (15)

Extract
Act II, Scene ii
Capulet's orchard

JULIET
O Romeo, Romeo! Wherefore art thou Romeo?
Deny thy father and refuse thy name;
Or, if thou wilt not, be but sworn my love,
And I'll no longer be a Capulet.
ROMEO
[Aside] Shall I hear more, or shall I speak at this?
JULIET
'Tis but thy name that is my enemy;
Thou art thyself, though not a Montague.
What's Montague? It is nor hand, nor foot,
Nor arm, nor face, nor any other part
Belonging to a man. O, be some other name!
What's in a name? That which we call a rose
By any other name would smell as sweet;
So Romeo would, were he not Romeo call'd,
Retain that dear perfection which he owes
Without that title. Romeo, doff thy name,
And for that name which is no part of thee
Take all myself.
ROMEO
I take thee at thy word:
Call me but love, and I'll be new baptized;
Henceforth I never will be Romeo.
JULIET
What man art thou that thus bescreen'd in night
So stumblest on my counsel?

ROMEO
By a name
I know not how to tell thee who I am:
My name, dear saint, is hateful to myself,
Because it is an enemy to thee;
Had I it written, I would tear the word.
JULIET
My ears have not yet drunk a hundred words
Of that tongue's utterance, yet I know the sound:
Art thou not Romeo and a Montague?
ROMEO
Neither, fair saint, if either thee dislike.
JULIET
How camest thou hither, tell me, and wherefore?
The orchard walls are high and hard to climb,
And the place death, considering who thou art,
If any of my kinsmen find thee here.
ROMEO
With love's light wings did I o'er-perch these walls;
For stony limits cannot hold love out,
And what love can do that dares love attempt;
Therefore thy kinsmen are no let to me.
JULIET
If they do see thee, they will murder thee.

and

b) How does Shakespeare explore the theme of love in another part of the play?   (15)

How well did you do for each question?

| 0–11 | Try again | 12–17 | Getting there | 18–23 | Good work | 24–30 | Excellent! |

Studying Drama

Studying Drama – Contemporary and Heritage

Another unit of your GCSE English Literature exam will require you to study a piece of drama other than Shakespeare. This could be a contemporary piece of drama such as Alan Bennett's *The History Boys* or a play from the English literary heritage, such as J. B. Priestley's *An Inspector Calls*.

This could be assessed in an exam, by controlled assessment or as a multi-modal response where you can present your findings using film, photos, presentations and re-enactments.

Conventions of Drama

When you are studying a novel or a poem, the writer will have used a variety of techniques to bring the text to life to allow you to visualise it in your mind. It will be structured in chapters, paragraphs or verses and dialogue will be laid out using the correct punctuation.

However, a piece of drama has its own conventions. It is structured in **acts** and **scenes**: an act is a large chunk or section and scenes are used to divide up the acts. At the start of a new act or new scene, you are usually given detailed **stage directions** which inform the actors what to do and how to do it. Stage directions can also give information about setting and props for the benefit of the director and designer. They can, however, choose to ignore these directions if they so wish. The script that you read is not a finished product – you could see it as a blueprint for a performance.

As you study the piece of drama in class, you will read the play and make detailed notes. However, you must remember that a play has been written to be performed and it is important that you try to see a performance of it.

Build Your Understanding

Whether you are watching a performance, taking part in a shared reading or annotating the text itself, there are key things that you should focus on:

- Stagecraft – these are the dramatic devices used to grab the audience's attention and convey the playwright's ideas – factors such as lighting, sets and props can all be part of the playwright's stagecraft.
- Characterisation – this is the way that the characters are portrayed – how has the playwright created a believable character? Has the writer included monologues or soliloquies to allow you to hear the character's thoughts and feelings? It is also important to look at the relationships between characters – how are these depicted? What do they reveal about the characters? You also need to think about the way that an actor or actress has represented the character. Different actors may play the same part in very different ways.
- Plot and structure – how have the events been organised? What techniques have been used to shape the action? How have the themes and ideas developed during the action?

Stage Directions

With any piece of drama that you study it is important that you pay close attention to the stage directions. Stage directions act as a set of instructions to the director and the actors and reveal important elements of the writer's stagecraft. They can also give you, as a reader, valuable insights into the playwright's intentions.

Look at the example below from J. B. Priestley's *An Inspector Calls*:

> The dining room of a fairly large suburban house, belonging to a prosperous manufacturer. It has good solid furniture of the period. At the moment they all have had a good dinner, are celebrating a special occasion and are pleased with themselves.

Even this short extract provides us with valuable information. We learn that the characters involved are wealthy and they start the play in a happy and self-satisfied mood. Their house is well furnished in a way that is typical of the time in which the play is set.

The setting is constant throughout the play as all of the action takes place there. The fact that we are invited into somebody's house is also important as it immediately creates a sense of intimacy – the audience is privy to what goes on behind closed doors.

The stage directions inform us that it is a 'heavily comfortable house' and that the lighting should be 'pink and intimate'. The lighting at this stage reflects the mood of the play – there is a 'rose tinted' aura on the stage and in the home.

Drama

❓ Test Yourself

❶ List at least four ways in which we can learn about characters in stage plays.

❷ What are stage directions?

★ Stretch Yourself

❶ Write a summary of the plot of the play you are studying in 100 words or fewer.

❷ Give examples of how the stage directions in the play you are studying provide information about its setting.

Character and Audience

Character

Stage directions reveal key information not only about setting, but also about character. For example, in the stage directions in *An Inspector Calls*, the writer, in giving a direction about the lighting, also informs us about the key character. When the Inspector arrives the lighting should become 'brighter and harder'.

This is an example of Priestley's stagecraft. It is a dramatic device used to show the importance of the Inspector – he enlightens the characters and the audience about what has been going on in the characters' lives.

Stage directions can also be found before the characters' dialogue. These provide important instructions about how words should be spoken and what **paralinguistic** features should be used to convey emotion. For example, the stage directions for the Inspector state that the character needs to create:

> ...an impression of massiveness, solidity and purposefulness... He speaks carefully, weightily, and has a disconcerting habit of looking hard at the person he addresses before actually speaking.

This information is clearly important for the person playing the part of the Inspector but when you are studying the text, it is as important as the words that the Inspector utters. It suggests a lot about the character. It is this kind of analysis that will be the focus of your assignment.

Reading Between the Lines

In addition to listening to what is being said and observing what is happening on stage, it is also important to think about the underlying messages and themes that are happening within the play. This is known as the **subtext**. In *An Inspector Calls* the Inspector is used not only as a dramatic device but also as a tool to highlight the playwright's views and beliefs. In one of his most important speeches in the play the Inspector tells the family and the audience:

> We don't live alone. We are members of one body. We are responsible for each other. And I tell you that the time will soon come when, if men will not learn that lesson, then they will be taught it in fire and blood and anguish. Good night.
> (Act three)

This quotation, taken from the Inspector's final lines, is full of rhetorical devices that attempt to persuade the audience and the characters that it is time to realise that their actions have consequences. It also effectively conveys Priestley's socialist message.

In addition, when you think about the subtext of this quotation in the context of both the time when the play is set and the time when it was first performed, the promise of 'fire, blood and anguish' is all the more chilling. The 1946 audience had just emerged from the Second World War and would have been conscious of the fact that the play is set only two years before the outbreak of the First World War.

Drama

Dramatic Irony

When the audience knows more than the characters this is called **dramatic irony**. This is a technique that many writers use as it helps highlight key messages and involve the audience. How is the quotation below, taken from *An Inspector Calls* an example of dramatic irony?

> A friend of mine went over this new liner last week – the Titanic – she sails next week – forty-six thousand eight hundred tons – forty-six thousand eight hundred tons – New York in five days – and every luxury – and unsinkable, absolutely unsinkable.
> (Act one)

Birling is talking to Gerald and Eric. The play is set in 1912 but was first performed in 1946. The audience watching the play – both then and now – would know that the Titanic did in fact sink.

It therefore becomes an effective example of dramatic irony that is symbolic of Birling's narrow mindedness and just as the Titanic sank, Birling's ideologies are also about to be washed away.

✓ Maximise Your Marks

When looking at any literary text you need to be able to identify techniques. Learning the correct terminology will impress the examiner. For example, a sudden turn of events in a piece of drama is called **coup de theatre**. Finding examples of such techniques and exploring them in detail will demonstrate a sophisticated response to the text. More important than knowing many such terms, however, is being able to demonstrate the effects the writer creates even if, in the heat of the exam, you forget its technical label.

? Test Yourself

1. What is meant by **coup de theatre**?
2. Can you identify a coup de theatre in the play you are studying and explain what triggers it?
3. What is subtext?

★ Stretch Yourself

1. Try to find three examples of dramatic irony in the play which you are studying.
   a) What does the audience know that the characters do not at these moments?
   b) What is the significance of these moments?

Analysing a Moving Image

Screen Works

Some exam boards require you to produce a piece of writing inspired by a moving image. This could be a film review of a Hollywood blockbuster or a comparison of a Shakespeare play or other drama text to a film adaptation.

You could be asked to discuss a film version of a popular piece of literature as a way of showing your understanding of the text. Some exam boards also ask you to look at a range of media texts such as film, TV, music videos and advertisements. In order to be able to write about this you need to have a basic understanding of moving image and media conventions.

🔆 Boost Your Memory

It is important to remember that analysing a moving image text is similar to analysing a piece of prose or non-fiction – you need to identify the techniques used and then explain their effect.

Build Your Understanding

If you were studying an extract from a piece of prose or a poem, you would comment on the writer's choice of language and the techniques that they use to get their message across.

✓ Maximise Your Marks

Two key terms to learn when looking at a moving image are connotation and denotation. Denotation is literally what you can see, and connotation is the implied meaning of what you can see. For example, look at the image below.

The denotation is the rose, whereas the connotation could be romance.

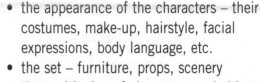

When looking at a moving image, you need to comment on how the director creates atmosphere and reveals information about genre and characters' thoughts and feelings.

In order to comment on how meaning has been portrayed you need to understand what is meant by mise-en-scene. Mise-en-scene is a French term that literally means 'put on stage' – when studying a moving image it refers to everything that you see in the frame or scene:

- the appearance of the characters – their costumes, make-up, hairstyle, facial expressions, body language, etc.
- the set – furniture, props, scenery
- the positioning of characters and objects
- lighting and colour
- sound
- camera angles and shots.

Drama

Sights and Sounds of Moving Images

When studying a moving image you need to be able to comment on the use of sound. This includes **dialogue** – the words spoken and the way that they are spoken – and **sound effects**. These can include **diegetic sounds**, which are sounds that are part of the action, for example the wind howling or birds tweeting, and **non-diegetic** sounds, which are added afterwards, such as voice overs and atmospheric music.

In addition to the camera angles, shots and movements it is also important to comment on lighting and colour as these can also be powerful tools. Colour, for example, can range from monochrome (black and white) to sepia, to deliberate colour effects to create impact. The film *Schindler's List*, for example, is shot mostly in monochrome. However, to create impact, colour is added to key sections. A little girl is seen wearing a red coat – the red contrasts with the black and white and the connotation of this is powerful as it implies danger and bloodshed.

Camera Angles and Movements

There are lots of different ways in which the camera can be moved. This is used to create specific effects and alter the way the audience responds to the image. Look at these examples:

- **Pan** – this is a slow movement which scans a scene horizontally. The camera is often placed on a tripod, which acts as a stationary point and then follows the object across the scene.
- **Tilt** – this is a movement which scans vertically.
- **Dolly** – this is sometimes called a tracking shot: the camera is placed on a moving vehicle (the dolly) and follows a moving figure or object.
- **Crane** – this provides a swooping action as the camera is placed on the end of a platform or jib. These are perfect for action scenes where a lot of swift movement is required.
- **Zoom** – this mechanical lens allows the camera to move close to or away from the object/action without moving itself.

- **Aerial** – this is an exciting shot usually taken from a helicopter. These shots are often used at the beginning of films to establish and set the scene. They can create a sense of drama and exhilaration.
- **Hand held** – this was first used effectively during the Second World War by news reporters and then later adapted for documentary producing a 'fly on the wall effect'. Hand-held camera actions are sometimes jerky and give a realistic effect. It was this technique that made films like *Blair Witch Project* a huge success.

Drama

? Test Yourself

1. Look at the ideas below – comment on the connotation of each.

Denotation	Connotation
Glasses	
Sunglasses	
Rose	
Sun	
Leaf	

★ Stretch Yourself

1. If you have watched a film or television adaptation of one of the texts you are studying for English Literature, make notes on any changes the director has made to the original story and the reasons for these changes.

Analysing a Moving Image

Camera Shots

Type of shot	Effect of different shots and impact upon audience
Extreme close up 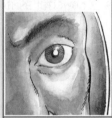	Extreme close ups and big close ups are used to show a significant part of an object – the view is often magnified beyond what the human eye would experience. This shot is often used for dramatic effect.
Close up 	Close ups are often used to focus on a face or object and show very little of the background. They draw your attention to important factors and can be used to show emotion.
Medium shots 	These shots usually appear to be from the waist up and are often used for dialogue scenes or to show some detail or action. They are often used when there is more than one person in the shot to show relationships between characters.
Long shot 	A long shot usually places the character within a background shot.
Very long shot 	A very or extreme long shot as it is sometimes known is often used as an establishing shot. These shots are used to show landscape and background and are there to give a general impression rather than detail.
Two shot 	Two shots have two people in view. They are used for dialogue scenes and to show relationships between characters.

Type of shot	Effect of different shots and impact upon audience
Over the shoulder shot 	These shots are also used during dialogue scenes and help involve the audience. You see the scene from the point of view of the character whose shoulder you are peering over.
Interview shot 	These shots are used during interview scenes and you usually have an eye level view – this is a neutral shot.
Moving subject 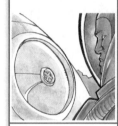	In this type of shot you follow the person in the scene and you see things as and when they do. They also show how a character responds to situations.
Tilted frame 	A tilted shot is used to create a sense of imbalance and is often used in horror films.
Low angle shot 	Low angle shots are used to look up at characters. This can make a character appear more powerful and help give a sense of confusion to the viewer, who becomes inferior to the person on the screen.
High angle shot 	This type of shot, also known as a bird's eye view shot, is shot from overhead and looks down on a character or place making them seem insignificant. It places the audience in a superior position.

Drama

Cuts and Edits

Once the footage for a film has been shot, the film director and editor then have to piece it all together. To get the most polished end product lots of shots are cut. Look at the list below to see the common edits that are used in films:

- **Straight cut** – this is the most common cut and is the one used to show continuity – it is the least noticeable as you are watching.
- **Dissolve** – this edit is often used to show the passing of time and to blend scenes of a similar nature. It is also used to create an eerie ambience.
- **Fade in / out** – this type of edit is used to indicate a movement in time or a new aspect of the story. Fades are also used at the end of the programme.
- **Wipe cut** – this edit sees one part of the scene being wiped away and a new scene introduced. It is often used in comedies or for humorous effect.
- **Jump cut** – this type of shot is used to make the audience focus on something quickly. It might show the passage of time without changing the location.
- **Montage** – this edit is used to show a number of shots in quick succession – it allows the director to give a lot of information in a small section of time.
- **Special FX** – as technology has developed so too have the special effects. Computer generated images (CGI), blue screen and 3D viewing are now common features.

✓ Maximise Your Marks

Remember to write your response in an analytical way – it is easy to get swept up in the plot of a film or television programme, but these tasks are analytical and so require you to interpret the effect of visual choices. A higher-grade answer will analyse, comment and explain the effectiveness of the film or programme, using correct media terminology.

❓ Test Yourself

1. What kind of shot or angle would you think was being used if you could see:
   a) a small figure climbing a fence in the distance?
   b) the expression on someone's face?
   c) a river winding its way through a valley?
   d) a man running through the streets as if you were chasing him?
   e) a shoe filling the scene?

⭐ Stretch Yourself

1. Pick a particularly effective scene from a film you have seen before (perhaps one you have studied in class) and make a note of the camera angles, shots and cuts used. Then explain the effect of each of them.

Practice Questions

 Complete these exam-style questions to test your understanding. Check your answers on pages 92–93. You will need to answer these questions on a separate piece of paper.

1 J.B. Priestley, *An Inspector Calls*

You are advised to spend about 45 minutes on this question.

How does J. B. Priestley present Inspector Goole in the play *An Inspector Calls*?

Comment on the following:

- How is the Inspector presented?

- How do the other characters respond to him?

- What methods does the playwright use to present this character?

- What are your thoughts on this character?

- How does Priestley use him to deliver a wider moral message? (20)

2 Diane Samuels, *Kindertransport*

You are advised to spend about 45 minutes on this question.

How are relationships between mothers and daughters presented in *Kindertransport*?

Comment on the following:

- The relationship between young Eva and her mother.

- Eva/Evelyn's relationship with her adoptive mother.

- Evelyn's relationship with her own daughter.

- Evelyn's reactions and attitudes when her 'real' mother reappears. (20)

3 Arthur Miller, *The Crucible*

You are advised to spend about 45 minutes on this question.

Towards the end of the play *The Crucible*, John Proctor says to Elizabeth that he is, 'no good man'. How does Miller present John Proctor? Is he a good man in your opinion?

Comment on the following:

- How is John Proctor presented?

- How do the other characters respond to him?

- What methods does the playwright use to present this character?

- What are your thoughts on this character?

- How does Miller use Proctor to explore the play's social and historical context? (20)

4 Willy Russell, *Blood Brothers*

You are advised to spend about 45 minutes on this question.

Compare the presentation of the two mothers in *Blood Brothers*.

Comment on the following:

- How is Mrs Johnstone presented?

- How is Mrs Lyons presented?

- What methods does the playwright use to present these characters?

- What are the differences and similarities between the two characters?

- How does Russell use the characters to explore issues about social class and background? (20)

How well did you do for each question?

| 0–7 | Try again | 8–11 | Getting there | 12–15 | Good work | 16–20 | Excellent! |

Novels and Short Stories

Studying Prose

Novels and short stories are both examples of **prose**.

Depending on your exam board, and the choices your teacher makes, you will either look at a novel or a collection of short stories. You might be studying a text from the English literary heritage, written over a hundred years ago, such as Charles Dickens' *Great Expectations* or Thomas Hardy's *Wessex Tales*. You could be studying a more contemporary text, such as *About a Boy* by Nick Hornby or a collection of stories by different authors collected in an anthology by the exam board.

Prose study can be assessed either as an exam topic or by controlled assessment. You might be allowed to have a clean copy of the text to refer to. However, this is not always the case – some exam boards will provide you with an extract from the text that you have been studying.

Whatever type of prose you are looking at, you will be required to comment on the genre, structure, style, characters, setting, themes, atmosphere, writer's use of language and in some cases, the social and historical context too.

Approaching the Text

If you are asked to look at an extract for your exam or for controlled assessment, you will need to consider these questions:
- What is the **purpose** of the extract?
- What **techniques** has the writer used to achieve that purpose?

On the following page is an extract taken from the first chapter of Charles Dickens' novel *Great Expectations*. Read through it carefully and think about what you learn from it and what effect is created.

You might like to think about:
- who the narrator is
- which characters are introduced and what you learn about them
- what setting or context is created
- what you notice about the writer's style
- whether it makes you want to read on, and why.

Prose

CHAPTER 1

My father's family name being Pirrip, and my Christian name Philip, my infant tongue could make of both names nothing longer or more explicit than Pip. So, I called myself Pip, and came to be called Pip.

I give Pirrip as my father's family name, on the authority of his tombstone and my sister – Mrs Joe Gargery, who married the blacksmith. As I never saw my father or my mother, and never saw any likeness of either of them (for their days were long before the days of photographs), my first fancies regarding what they were like, were unreasonably derived from their tombstones. The shape of the letters on my father's gave me an odd idea that he was a square, stout, dark man, with curly black hair. From the character and turn of the inscription, 'Also Georgiana Wife of the above', I drew a childish conclusion that my mother was freckled and sickly. To five little stone lozenges, each about a foot and a half long, which were arranged in a neat row beside their grave, and were sacred to the memory of five little brothers of mine – who gave up trying to get a living, exceedingly early in that universal struggle – I am indebted for a belief I religiously entertained that they had all been born on their backs with their hands in their trousers-pockets, and had never taken them out in this state of existence.

Ours was the marsh country, down by the river, within, as the river wound, twenty miles of the sea. My first most vivid and broad impression of the identity of things, seems to me to have been gained on a memorable raw afternoon towards evening. At such a time I found out for certain, that this bleak place overgrown with nettles was the churchyard; and that Philip Pirrip, late of this parish, and also Georgiana wife of the above, were dead and buried; and that Alexander, Bartholomew, Abraham, Tobias, and Roger, infant children of the aforesaid, were also dead and buried; and that the dark flat wilderness beyond the churchyard, intersected with dykes and mounds and gates, with scattered cattle feeding on it, was the marshes; and that the low leaden line beyond, was the river; and that the distant savage lair from which the wind was rushing, was the sea; and that the small bundle of shivers growing afraid of it all and beginning to cry, was Pip.

'Hold your noise!' cried a terrible voice, as a man started up from among the graves at the side of the church porch. 'Keep still, you little devil, or I'll cut your throat!'

A fearful man, all in coarse grey, with a great iron on his leg. A man with no hat, and with broken shoes, and with an old rag tied round his head. A man who had been soaked in water, and smothered in mud, and lamed by stones, and cut by flints, and stung by nettles, and torn by briars; who limped, and shivered, and glared and growled; and whose teeth chattered in his head as he seized me by the chin.

'O! Don't cut my throat, sir,' I pleaded in terror. 'Pray don't do it, sir.'

'Tell us your name!' said the man. 'Quick!'

'Pip, sir.'

'Once more,' said the man, staring at me. 'Give it mouth!'

'Pip. Pip, sir.'

'Show us where you live,' said the man. 'Pint out the place!'

I pointed to where our village lay, on the flat in-shore among the alder-trees and pollards, a mile or more from the church.

The man, after looking at me for a moment, turned me upside down, and emptied my pockets. There was nothing in them but a piece of bread. When the church came to itself – for he was so sudden and strong that he made it go head over heels before me, and I saw the steeple under my feet – when the church came to itself, I say, I was seated on a high tombstone, trembling, while he ate the bread ravenously.

'You young dog,' said the man, licking his lips, 'what fat cheeks you ha' got.'

I believe they were fat, though I was at that time undersized for my years, and not strong.

'Darn me if I couldn't eat em,' said the man, with a threatening shake of his head, 'and if I han't half a mind to't!'

I earnestly expressed my hope that he wouldn't, and held tighter to the tombstone on which he had put me; partly, to keep myself upon it; partly, to keep myself from crying.

The main purpose of this extract is to introduce the novel's protagonist to the reader and to establish the sad plot of the orphan Pip.

Dickens does this successfully through clever characterisation, an unwelcoming setting that creates an eerie ambience and a range of literary techniques that create drama and tension.

This first chapter succeeds in establishing setting, tone and character. There is immediate drama and the entire plot that follows is a consequence of the events that take place in this first chapter.

? Test Yourself

1. What do we learn about Pip and his family from this extract?

2. What do we learn about the setting from this extract?

★ Stretch Yourself

1. What difference does the use of the first person narrator make to your experience of reading this extract?

Literary Techniques

Atmosphere and Mood

The **atmosphere** and **mood** of a text are very important and are created through several different techniques. The atmosphere and mood of a text are closely linked to its genre. However, it is the combination of the following factors that help the writer create the desired 'ambience'.

Diction – this means the writer's choice of words.

In the *Great Expectations* extract on page 65, words are used to create a variety of moods. For example, when Dickens wants to create sympathy he uses emotive language:

> To five little stone lozenges, each about a foot and a half long, which were arranged in a neat row beside their grave, and were sacred to the memory of five little brothers of mine – who gave up trying to get a living, exceedingly early in that universal struggle...

Setting – this is also an effective way of creating mood and atmosphere. The cemetery is no place for a seven year old boy to be. This helps create an eerie and sinister atmosphere that fits the scene perfectly as an escaped convict appears from out of the marshes.

Narrative viewpoint – in the extract, Pip introduces himself to us and the use of first-person narrative allows us to see things through his eyes. This is an effective way of creating mood and atmosphere because we see things through his eyes – the chapter is even more terrifying as the events taking place are happening to a child.

Characters – the choice of characters can affect our reaction to the atmosphere and mood. In the extract from *Great Expectations* on page 65 Dickens juxtaposes two contrasting characters – we have an escaped convict and an innocent child. We immediately sympathise with Pip the young boy: 'I never saw my father or my mother'. As an orphan he appears particularly vulnerable; however, we also get to see a helpless side of the convict and then we begin to form an attachment to him as well. This is particularly effective in this story as *Great Expectations* is about the expectations of both characters. Even the names that Dickens gives to his characters are significant: Pip sounds like a seed and the novel does see Pip grow from a young, working class boy into a gentleman. A novel which charts the growth and education of the protagonist is called a **bildungsroman**.

Tone – this is closely related to atmosphere and is particularly important as it reflects the attitude of the writer. In *Great Expectations*, Dickens is using Pip as a way of looking at Victorian life. Dickens was saddened by the way that poor people were treated because of his own experiences and his exploration of these ideas in the text creates a sombre and reflective mood. In the extract on page 65 the gloomy tone created by the description 'this bleak place overgrown with nettles' is combined with the black humour of the young Pip's reflections on his dead family.

Identifying the Writer's Craft

The *Great Expectations* extract is a very good example of a text that is full of literary techniques. All of the following can be found in the text:

- symbolism
- powerful adjectives
- emotive language
- personification
- pathetic fallacy
- accent and dialogue
- repetition
- powerful verbs
- onomatopoeia
- alliteration
- humour

Humour – 'what fat cheeks you ha' got'

Powerful verbs – 'glared', 'seized'

Accent and dialogue – 'Give it mouth!'

Onomatopoeia – 'growled', 'chattered'

Emotive language – 'small bundle of shivers growing afraid of it all'

Build Your Understanding

When you are looking at a piece of literature and analysing it, remember that if you can interpret the language used in more than one way, you are beginning to analyse in detail which will get you higher marks. For example, in the following quotation Dickens creates both humour and fear:

> 'You young dog', said the man, licking his lips, 'what fat cheeks you ha' got.'

Pip would clearly be terrified by the convict's observation as it suggests that he wants to eat the boy. However, this quotation also sounds like a well known fairy tale and therefore the convict's speech seems almost comical – he is being painted as the big, bad wolf in 'Little Red Riding Hood'.

To gain a high grade, your analysis will need to be sophisticated and you will need to imaginatively select quotations and go beyond the obvious. You will need to consider unusual interpretations and explore different layers of meaning.

When you are selecting quotations it is also important to think about how long your quotation is. It is better to have a short quotation than a long one. However, there are occasions when it is necessary to quote a larger section; if this is the case, then as a rule of thumb, your explanation should usually be about three times the length of your quotation.

? Test Yourself

1. Find examples of the following literary techniques in the extract from *Great Expectations*:
   a) repetition
   b) dialogue
   c) powerful adjectives
   d) alliteration
   e) personification

★ Stretch Yourself

1. Explain the differences between Pip's speech and the speech of the stranger. What do these differences tell us about the two characters?

Exploring Culture in Prose

Culture

Culture can be a difficult concept to understand because there are so many different aspects that make up a person's culture. You could go away on holiday to somewhere exotic and find that in many ways the way of life there is similar to your own, but you might also find significant cultural differences.

The ingredients that contribute to our cultural identity can include: accent, dialect, language, food, dress, music, literature, politics, education, religion, work, attitude and manners. Some differences in culture are the result of geographical location, but some are because of history. As time changes and society evolves, so too do aspects of culture. Your task will be to focus on how the writers of the texts that you are studying have created a sense of culture in their writing.

✓ Maximise Your Marks

You will gain higher marks if you refer to specific cultural elements. One of the most enjoyable things about reading a text from another culture is the way that you learn about another way of life. Being able to pick out similarities and differences between cultures, discuss their impact on characters and themes, and select evidence from the text to back up what you say will impress the examiner.

Types of Text

For your exam or controlled assessment you will be studying an example of prose that explores a culture different from your own; an example of 'global' literature that has been written in English. Among the texts that you might be studying are John Steinbeck's *Of Mice and Men*, set in 1930s California, and Meera Syal's *Anita and Me*, a story that looks at the experience of a young girl living in England but born to Indian parents. Other set texts include novels and stories set in Africa, Asia and South America.

This revision guide will look at *Anita and Me* and *Of Mice and Men* and explore how these texts depict culture, looking at context, character, themes, and textual analysis. These skills are transferable to any of the prose texts that you might study.

You will need to be able to explain how life is depicted in the text that you are studying, thinking about cultural similarities and differences. Whether you are assessed in an exam or by means of controlled assessment, you will have to analyse and explore the text in detail, paying particular attention to the writer's language. You will also be expected to comment on the **social and historical context** of the prose. The text could be concerned with important issues like racial prejudice or attitudes to gender. You will need to be able to comment on the implications of these themes and ideas and read between the lines.

Build Your Understanding

Look at the extract below taken from *Anita and Me* by Meera Syal:

> But if Tollington was a footnote in the book of the Sixties, then my family and friends were the squashed flies in the spine. According to the newspapers and television, we simply did not exist. If a brown or black face ever did appear on TV, it stopped us all in our tracks. 'Daljit! Quick!' Papa would call, and we would crowd round and coo over the walk-on in some detective series, some long-suffering actor in a gaudy costume with a goodness-gracious-me accent ('So Mr Templar, you speak fluent Hindustani too! But that won't stop me stealing the secret formula for my country from where I will soon rule the world! Heh heh heh…') and welcome him into our house like a long-lost relative. But these occasional minor celebrities never struck me as real; they were someone else's version of Indian, far too exaggerated and exotic to be believable. Sometimes I wondered if the very act of shutting our front door transported us onto another planet, where non-related elders were called Aunties and Uncles and talked in rapid Punjabi, which their children understood but answered back in broad Black Country slang, where we ate food with our fingers and discussed family feuds happening five thousand miles away, where manners were so courtly that a raised eyebrow could imply an insult, where sensibilities were so finely tuned that an advert featuring a woman in a bikini could clear a room.

Anita and Me is about Meena, an English Punjabi girl living in a fictional village in the Midlands in the 1970s. As this text is set in the United Kingdom you might assume that it is not a good example of a cultural text because you are familiar with British culture. However, this novel illustrates how multicultural the United Kingdom is and teaches you that cultural differences do not only exist because of geography. In your controlled assessment or exam, you might be asked to look at what you learn about Meena's experience of living between two cultures from an extract like this. In response to this question you might comment on:

- How the writer describes how Indian families behave in their own homes.
- What the writer suggests about the impact of the media on the Indian community.
- What the references to Meena's extended family tell you about attitudes to family and culture in the Indian community.
- What the differences are between the speech of adults and children.
- What differences between British and Indian culture are shown in this extract.

❓ Test Yourself

1. What is meant by the term 'multicultural society'?

2. What differences between British and Indian culture are shown in the extract from *Anita and Me* above?

⭐ Stretch Yourself

1. Think about the text you are studying for this unit of work. Where and when is it set? Which aspects of the cultural setting strike you as being different from your own culture and background? Make a list of examples.

Culture in *Of Mice and Men*

Prose

Context

Of Mice and Men was written by John Steinbeck in 1937 and deals with the subject of the disempowered poor searching for a better life.

Steinbeck was inspired by the **Great Depression** that tore through America after the Wall Street Crash of 1929; it took 10 years for the American economy to recover and during this time almost a third of the population were unemployed. Consequently, many workers travelled around the country looking for jobs. A lot of people headed to California hoping to buy land, set up their own farms and lead a better life. **George** and **Lennie** are characters who aspire to this and the novel examines how they strive to achieve their dream.

Setting the Scene

The novel starts with a vivid description of an idyllic scene on a hot day – two men enter the scene and we are introduced to the protagonists, George and Lennie. The stillness described at the start of the novel contrasts dramatically with the tension and conflict that occurs in the rest of the text. Set beneath the Gabilan Mountains, this first chapter evocatively depicts rural California. The rest of the novel takes place on the Tyler Ranch, giving Steinbeck the opportunity to explore the life of an itinerant worker. Each chapter starts with Steinbeck setting the scene, much like stage directions at the start of a new scene in a piece of drama; the dialogue that then takes place between the characters provides an insight into the life and culture of the characters. Interestingly, the novel goes full circle and the final chapter ends at the place where the novel started. This can be seen as a reminder of the timelessness and supremacy of nature – our natural world has to endure human life and the trouble that we bring to it.

Characters

Through the characters in the novel Steinbeck explores status in 1930s America. There is an interesting hierarchy of power shown in the text. At the top of this hierarchy is the owner of the ranch, the boss man who employs the other characters. However, he is a minor character. His son, **Curley**, who we would assume is powerful because of his father's position, is not regarded highly by the men, or the reader. **Slim**, a 'jerk line skinner', is a hard working man, described as 'the prince of the ranch' and as 'having a gravity in his manner and a quiet so profound that all talk stopped when he spoke'. Slim is perceived to be more powerful because of his personality and professionalism.

Yet it is the lower end of the social ladder that really depicts cultural elements of 1930s America. **Curley's wife**, **Crooks**, **Candy** and Lennie are the least powerful characters – they each represent a minority within American society. Let's focus on Curley's wife and see how Steinbeck uses her to explore cultural issues.

Even before we meet Curley's wife, Candy informs George and Lennie that she is a 'tart' and then when she enters the bunk room looking for her husband, Steinbeck presents her as trouble, using light as a symbol of the trouble that she 'may' cause:

> Both men glanced up, for the rectangle of sunshine in the doorway was cut off.

Her presence literally prevents light from entering the bunkhouse; the darkness that is associated with her creates a sense of foreboding. Steinbeck describes Curley's wife's appearance in the sense of what she is wearing and how she is made up. Curley's wife is 'ornamental'; she isn't even given a name. The shoes that she wears are 'red mules'; the colour red here can again be seen as a symbol of danger.

Characters (cont.)

The portrayal of women in *Of Mice and Men* is unflattering; George has no desire for a female companion and berates Lennie for having his head turned by Curley's wife. Steinbeck portrays Curley's wife as flirtatious and she is cruel to Crooks, threatening to have him lynched. Yet Steinbeck also portrays her in a sympathetic light. She is married to a brutish man and her life is totally unfulfilled. Just before her death, she voices to Lennie and the reader, her dream of stardom and her hopes of a better life. For women like Curley's wife, marriage and children would have been their only option, especially in masculine communities like the one at the ranch. The fact that Steinbeck does not give Curley's wife a name is also important because her anonymity highlights how insignificant she is.

Themes

Themes are the important ideas and issues that run through a text. For this particular task, the themes will be important because the writer will be exploring themes connected to cultural elements. In *Of Mice and Men* we see themes of:

Human nature – regardless of our culture, humans all share similar emotions. *Of Mice and Men* looks at these through people's hopes and fears.

Friendship – the friendship of migrant workers George and Lennie might be thought unusual. However, it is their friendship which is perhaps the most striking theme in the novel and it has a profound impact on the readers.

Dreams – in particular, dreams are shown in this text in relation to the idea of the 'American Dream'. Culturally, this links to American history and a person's desire for happiness and freedom regardless of the factors that stand in their way. However, the reality of this is not always the case.

Role of women – as discussed above with regards to Curley's wife, women are presented in a negative light, showing attitudes towards women that might be typical of the time.

Minorities – as with gender issues, the novel also looks at ideas associated with race, age and disabilities. The weaker characters are all hindered by these factors.

Work and power – the whole story is very masculine and this is shown through the type of work that the characters do and their histories. This again reveals a lot about the nature of employment at the time in this part of the world.

When you are writing about themes for this aspect of your course, you will need to demonstrate your ability to trace these themes throughout the text and explore them with regards to culture. What do they tell you about life for the characters? How has society changed?

✓ Maximise Your Marks

To gain higher marks, you need to relate these themes to other aspects of the texts, such as character, voice, language, structure and form. The theme of dreams, for example, can be related to many of the characters. They all have different dreams, but their dreams contain similarities too. They all want to be free from the constraints of society.

❓ Test Yourself

1. Why does Steinbeck not give Curley's wife a name?

2. What is the significance of the novel starting and ending at the same place?

⭐ Stretch Yourself

1. Think about the text you are studying for this unit. What do you think are its main themes? How do these relate to its cultural context?

Practice Questions

 Complete these exam-style questions to test your understanding. Check your answers on page 94. You will need to answer these questions on a separate piece of paper.

Check your answers on page 94.

1 **Prose from the English Literary Heritage**

You should spend about 45 minutes on this question.

Pride and Prejudice by Jane Austen

What do you learn about the character of Darcy from the extract below
(taken from Chapter 11 of *Pride and Prejudice*)? (20)

> 'Certainly,' replied Elizabeth —'there are such people, but I hope I am not one of them. I hope I never ridicule what is wise or good. Follies and nonsense, whims and inconsistencies do divert me, I own, and I laugh at them whenever I can. —But these, I suppose, are precisely what you are without.'
>
> 'Perhaps that is not possible for anyone. But it has been the study of my life to avoid those weaknesses which often expose a strong understanding to ridicule.'
>
> 'Such as vanity and pride.'
>
> 'Yes, vanity is a weakness indeed. But pride —where there is a real superiority of mind, pride will be always under good regulation.'
>
> Elizabeth turned away to hide a smile.
>
> 'Your examination of Mr Darcy is over, I presume,' said Miss Bingley; —'and pray what is the result?'
>
> 'I am perfectly convinced by it that Mr Darcy has no defect. He owns it himself without disguise.'
>
> 'No' —said Darcy, 'I have made no such pretension. I have faults enough, but they are not, I hope, of understanding. My temper I dare not vouch for. —It is I believe too little yielding — certainly too little for the convenience of the world. I cannot forget the follies and vices of others so soon as I ought, nor their offences against myself. My feelings are not puffed about with every attempt to move them. My temper would perhaps be called resentful. —My good opinion once lost is lost for ever.'
>
> 'That is a failing indeed!' —cried Elizabeth. 'Implacable resentment is a shade in a character. But you have chosen your fault well. —I really cannot laugh at it. You are safe from me.'
>
> 'There is, I believe, in every disposition a tendency to some particular evil, a natural defect, which not even the best education can overcome.'
>
> 'And your defect is a propensity to hate every body.'
>
> 'And yours,' he replied with a smile, 'is wilfully to misunderstand them.'

Prose

❷ Exploring Prose from Different Cultures

You should spend about 45 minutes on this question.

Of Mice and Men by John Steinbeck

Explain the importance of Curley's wife in the novel. In your response you must consider:

- Her relationship with her husband Curley.

- How the men describe and treat her.

- Her hopes and dreams.

You may also include other examples that you think are important. Use evidence from the text to support your answer. (20)

❸ Exploring Prose from Different Cultures

You should spend about 45 minutes on this question.

To Kill A Mockingbird by Harper Lee

Discuss the presentation of Atticus as a hero and a father in the novel.

You might consider:

- His relationship with his children.

- What his children think about him.

- What other people in the community think about him.

- What is meant by 'a good father'?

- What is meant by 'a hero'?

Use evidence from the text to support your answer. (20)

How well did you do for each question?

| 0–7 | Try again | 8–11 | Getting there | 12–15 | Good work | 16–20 | Excellent! |

Poetic Form and Features

Poetry

Poetry could be assessed in an exam or as part of a controlled assessment. There will be a written response to a collection of poems that you have studied beforehand – both modern poetry and literary heritage poetry. Some exam boards also require you to write a response to a poem that you have not seen before.

By now, after all of the work that you have done with other texts, you should be skilled at analysing aspects of language and structure.

This is exactly the same for your work on poetry – you need to demonstrate your understanding of the poem's meaning and explore the ways that the poet gets that meaning across. As with all of the other texts that you have studied, there are key techniques that poets use to express meaning. When you are studying poetry, you will need to read the poem several times and ask yourself some simple questions:
- How does the poem sound?
- What is the shape of the poem?
- What is the poem about?
- Why did the poet write the poem?
- Are there any important messages in the poem?
- What techniques has the poet used?

Poetic Form

The **form** of a poem is the way that it is written. There are many different types of poetry that vary in shape and size – poets either maintain the conventions of these forms or they experiment with them to achieve different effects and create different meanings. Some common forms of poetry that you might be familiar with are: sonnet, haiku, ballad, free verse, narrative poem and limerick. Each of these has its own conventions and when you are studying poetry it is important to recognise these. Structurally poems will differ, but when talking about poems it is important to refer to their sections as **verses** or **stanzas**.

Aural Imagery

Poets use many techniques to express meaning within their poetry. During the Renaissance period, poets used elaborate techniques to show how skilful they were. Poems are often written to be read aloud. The techniques below are all examples of sound effects used in poetry.

Alliteration – when a series of words begin with the same consonant sounds:
> He clasps the crag with crooked hands.
> (Alfred Lord Tennyson, *The Eagle*)

Assonance – repetition of vowel sounds:
> 'Tis visible silence, still as the hour-glass.
> (Dante Gabriel Rossetti, *Silent Noon*)

Discordant and euphonious sounds – harsh (discordant) and pleasing (euphonious) sounds used to achieve opposite effects:
> Mewling and puking in the nurse's arms.
> (Shakespeare, *As You Like It*)

> The cloud-capp'd towers, the gorgeous palaces.
> (Shakespeare, *The Tempest*)

Onomatopoeia – words that sound like their meaning: clang; fizz; cackle.

Rhyme – word endings that have a similar sound:
> I shot an arrow in the air,
> It fell to earth,
> I knew not where.
> (Henry Longfellow, *The Arrow and the Song*)

Figurative Imagery

There are also techniques that are used to create visual effects.

Simile – a comparison using the words 'like' or 'as'; a common figure of speech used in poetry. Similes help readers create pictures in their minds:

And ice, mast-high, came floating by,
As green as emerald.
(Samuel Taylor Coleridge, *The Rime of the Ancient Mariner*)

Metaphor – a metaphor is similar to a simile in that it also compares things. However, the comparison is implied and does not use 'like' or 'as'. Metaphorical language can be elaborate and used as a dramatic device. Poems often have extended metaphors, where the metaphor is developed throughout the poem. This type of metaphor that becomes central to the poem is called a **conceit**:

Was it the proud full sail of his great verse,
Bound for the prize of all too precious you.
(Shakespeare, *Sonnet 86*)

Personification – personification is where inanimate objects or ideas are given human qualities. It is a subtle way of allowing the reader to visualise elements of the poem:

Death, be not proud. (John Donne)

Symbolism – symbolism is used to provide meaning to the poem beyond what is actually being described. The narrative of the poem can be thought of as one level, while the symbolism of certain things in the poem act on another level to enhance the meaning. Symbols can be objects, characters, colours and figures used to represent abstract ideas or concepts:

Little Lamb, who made thee?
(William Blake, *The Lamb*)

Pathetic fallacy – pathetic fallacy is similar to personification, but is usually connected to weather and atmosphere; it refers to how the weather and elements of nature are used to reflect the mood:

Sudden from heaven like a weeping cloud.
(John Keats, *Ode on Melancholy*)

Oxymoron – two contradictory terms placed together: 'loving hate'; 'bitter sweet'.

Build Your Understanding

You might also refer to techniques that are concerned with the poem's structure, such as enjambment and caesura.

Enjambment is where a line is not end-stopped and runs on to another line. It is often used to aid rhythm and create a specific effect, for example reflecting continuity of thought. The opposite of this, when lines end with a full stop, is called end-stopping.

Caesura, which literally means 'cutting', is when punctuation is used to indicate a pause within a line of poetry, perhaps helping to emphasise particular words or giving the impression of a lack of order and continuity.

? Test Yourself

1. Which techniques are used in the following lines?
   a) 'Pale, beyond porch and portal.'
   b) '...and heard the Mountain's slumbrous voice at intervals.'
   c) 'I wandered lonely as a cloud.'
   d) 'What! Must I hold a candle to my shames?'

★ Stretch Yourself

1. Look at the following extract from a poem by John Keats called *Endymion*. What is the effect of the poet's use of enjambment, end-stopping and caesura?

   A thing of beauty is a joy forever:
   Its loveliness increases; it will never
   Pass into nothingness; but still will keep
   A bower quiet for us, and a sleep
   Full of sweet dreams, and health, and
   quiet breathing.

Poetry

Poetry Comparison

Comparing Poems

Most exam boards will ask you to compare at least two poems and you will make comparisons of the following things:

- form, structure and style
- themes, ideas and issues
- language techniques

You will need to talk about both the similarities and the differences. You can approach your comparison in a number of ways. You could choose to look at one poem in detail and then use it to make links to the other poems that you are looking at or you could talk about an element of one poem and then immediately refer to the other poem. The flowchart below shows you how to plan a response to a comparative essay question.

✓ Maximise Your Marks

If you can learn to compare poems using Model B below (looking at them together rather than in separate paragraphs) you will have acquired a skill that should help you gain higher marks.

Choose the question that you feel most confident about.

↓

Highlight key words in the question that you can refer back to throughout your response.

↓

Make a plan – think about the key areas that you will need to cover.

Model A	**Model B**
Explore key points from the first poem.	Explore a key point in both poems e.g. Both poems use a central metaphor, for example in the first poem, the poet suggests... whereas in the second poem...
Explore key points from the second poem.	Explore further key points in both poems e.g. Another similarity between the poems is...
Make comparisons between the two poems.	Explore contrasting ideas within the two poems.

Concluding paragraph – refer back to the question and summarise your main ideas.

Build Your Understanding

You will be writing an analytical essay so you may use the P.E.E. method for the main body of your essay. Your explorations are where you will pick up most of your marks so you must make sure that your analysis is detailed. Talk about how the poem made you feel and the effect of the technique that you have identified. To show that you are comparing, you will have to use connective phrases to link your paragraphs:

- Similarities – in the same way, similarly, also.
- Differences – whereas, however, unlike, in contrast, on the other hand.

To get the best possible grade that you can, when you are using the P.E.E. method try to expand your paragraph into a P.E.E.E.E. paragraph:

P	Make a point about the quotation or poem that you are writing about.

E	Choose a relevant quotation.

E	Explain the quotation and in your exploration of the quotation, make a link to another part of the poem or another poem that you are comparing it to.

E	Choose a quotation that links to the comparison that you have just made.

E	Explore the second quotation and the importance of it by itself, but also in relation to your earlier point and the poem/poems as a whole.

✓ **Maximise Your Marks**

When analysing poetry and identifying techniques, try to identify sophisticated techniques such as caesura and enjambment, or oxymoron and assonance. But remember that simply 'spotting' these techniques will not be enough for A or A* candidates. You must be able to explain their effect on you, the reader. The examiner will be impressed by your knowledge and understanding of more complex techniques.

William Blake's *The Lamb* opens with two questions:

> Little Lamb, who made thee?
> Dost thou know who made thee?

It would appear that Blake, or 'the child' with whose voice he is speaking, is asking the question so that he himself can answer it. The opening stanza of 'The Tyger' also asks a question:

> What immortal hand or eye
> Could frame thy fearful symmetry?

The question is similar, but in this poem no answer is given. Whereas, in *The Lamb* we are confidently told that the same God made both the child and the lamb, here there is no such certainty. At the end of the poem, the poet still has no answer to the mystery of whether the tiger and the lamb were both made by the same being.

Useful Phrases

When you are analysing different poems, have a selection of stock phrases up your sleeve to help get you going:

- The poet makes the reader feel…
- The use of the word '_____' is effective because…
- Alliteration / Personification / Metaphors, etc. are used by the poet to create a feeling of…
- The poet implies…
- When the poet says '_____', this is symbolic of…

? **Test Yourself**

❶ List five areas you might look at when comparing poems.

❷ Give three examples of connective phrases you could use when discussing similarities between two poems.

⭐ **Stretch Yourself**

❶ Use the P.E.E.E.E. model above to compare one aspect of two poems you have studied.

Practice Questions

 Complete these exam-style questions to test your understanding. Check your answers on pages 94–95. You will need to answer these questions on a separate piece of paper.

Unseen Poetry

1 You are advised to spend about 30 minutes on this question.

Read the poem below, *No!* by Thomas Hood

How does the poet convey a sense of the season and his feelings about it?

Comment on:

- The description of what it is like in November.
- The effect of the weather on people.
- The language the poet uses.
- The structure of the poem.
- Anything else that you think is important. (20)

No sun--no moon!
No morn--no noon!
No dawn--no dusk--no proper time of day--
No sky--no earthly view--
No distance looking blue--

No road--no street--no 't'other side the way'--
No end to any Row--
No indications where the Crescents go--

No top to any steeple--
No recognitions of familiar people--
No courtesies for showing 'em--
No knowing 'em!

No travelling at all--no locomotion
No inkling of the way--no notion
'No go' by land or ocean--

No mail--no post--
No news from any foreign coast--
No Park--no Ring--no afternoon gentility--
No company--no nobility--

No warmth, no cheerfulness, no healthful ease,
No comfortable feel in any member--
No shade, no shine, no butterflies, no bees,
No fruits, no flowers, no leaves, no birds,
November!

2 You are advised to spend about 45 minutes on this question.

Look at the poem by Wilfred Owen below. Compare how war is shown in *Dulce et Decorum est* with one other poem that you have studied.

Remember to compare:

* War in the poems.
* Ways in which war is presented.

(20)

Bent double, like old beggars under sacks,
Knock-kneed, coughing like hags, we cursed through sludge,
Till on the haunting flares we turned our backs
And towards our distant rest began to trudge.
Men marched asleep. Many had lost their boots
But limped on, blood-shod. All went lame; all blind;
Drunk with fatigue; deaf even to the hoots
Of tired, outstripped Five-Nines that dropped behind.

Gas! Gas! Quick, boys!--- An ecstasy of fumbling,
Fitting the clumsy helmets just in time;
But someone still was yelling out and stumbling
And flound'ring like a man in fire or lime...
Dim, through the misty panes and thick green light
As under a green sea, I saw him drowning.

In all my dreams, before my helpless sight,
He plunges at me, guttering, choking, drowning.

If in some smothering dreams you too could pace
Behind the wagon that we flung him in,
And watch the white eyes writhing in his face,
His hanging face, like a devil's sick of sin;
If you could hear, at every jolt, the blood
Come gargling from the froth-corrupted lungs,
Obscene as cancer, bitter as the cud
Of vile, incurable sores on innocent tongues,---
My friend, you would not tell with such high zest
To children ardent for some desperate glory,
The old Lie: Dulce et decorum est
Pro patria mori.

How well did you do for each question?

| 0–7 | Try again | 8–11 | Getting there | 12–15 | Good work | 16–20 | Excellent! |

Presenting Information and Ideas

Speaking and Listening Task

You will be expected to prepare and perform at least three oral responses as part of your controlled assessment. These tasks will contribute 20 per cent to your overall mark.

The tasks may include the following:
- An individual presentation.
- A group discussion.
- A dramatic performance/role play.
- A multi-modal response.

Preparing for Your Speech

The stress of a speaking and listening task can be minimised by research and groundwork. Choose a topic that you are interested in and research your topic thoroughly. Think about the materials that you will use to enhance your speech – are you able to use ICT facilities or index cards to guide you through and help engage your audience? If you are performing in role can you use props to help make your character more believable?

Another important factor is understanding your audience. What will be an appropriate speaking style? Will you need to adapt your language, content or style to suit your audience?

Presenting Your Speech

Giving a speech is a great way of exploring an issue that you feel passionately about. It is important that you structure your talk well:
- **Introduction** – Greet your audience and explain what you will be talking about.
- **Detail** – Share your information but be careful not to bore your audience. Think quality not quantity when it comes to the main points.
- **Conclusion** – Bring your speech to a close. Try to end on an interesting note and involve your audience by inviting comments and questions.

There will be people watching you – your classmates and your teacher – and it is your job to grab their attention and make them listen to what you are saying. To do this make sure that you:
- Use an appropriate register – Standard English and formal language – no 'Yo!' or 'Innit!'

- Speak clearly and fluently.
- Vary your tone for emphasis.
- Make eye-contact and do not read from prompts.
- Smile – put your audience at ease and it will also help you relax.
- Speak at an appropriate pace.
- Appear confident – hold your head high, project your voice and do not fidget.

✓ Maximise Your Marks

To deliver your presentation effectively, you have to appear confident on the outside, even if you are not confident on the inside. Make regular eye contact and use body language to portray confidence. Try using props and visual aids to illustrate and enhance your speech.

Build Your Understanding

The best speeches are memorable – first impressions mean a lot. When politicians and celebrities speak, their dialogue has usually been crafted by an expert. You can mirror this by using a range of rhetorical techniques in your speech, such as:

- Rhetorical questions – 'When was the last time a film made you cry?'
- Emotive language – 'It is outrageous that all over the world people are suffering because of the harsh reality of climate change.'
- Use of pronouns – 'People like you and I can make a difference.'
- Hyperbole – 'If we don't act soon there will be no tomorrow.'

✓ Maximise Your Marks

Choose a subject that you know you can talk about at length and answer questions about. However, remember that the easy choice will not always give you the best mark. An examiner will be more impressed by, and give credit for, the confident management of complex material. Show the examiner that you have researched and developed your content by including evidence to back up your points.

🔆 Boost Your Memory

Rehearse your speech – talk to the mirror, to parents or friends. It does not matter how well written your speech is if it is not delivered well. If you want to review your own performance, have a go at recording yourself and then judge your own performance – what grade would you award yourself? How could your performance be improved?

First and Final Impressions

How you start sets the tone and prepares the audience for the rest of your speech. An attention grabbing speech will have a memorable beginning. Play with your audience's emotions. Try using a memorable quotation, a powerful statistic or even a joke.

You also need to leave a lasting impression. Once you have summarised your argument, you should ask your audience if they have any questions. It is a good idea to try to be prepared for these and have answers to likely questions rehearsed in advance.

❓ Test Yourself

1. List five things you could use (apart from your voice!) to make your individual presentation more effective.

⭐ Stretch Yourself

1. Practise speaking without notes for three minutes on a subject of your choice. Record your speech. When you play it back note areas for improvement and repeat the exercise.

Group Discussion and Drama

Speaking and Listening

Group Discussion

When you are discussing a topic you are demonstrating three key skills – your ability to **communicate** your ideas, your ability to **listen** to what others have said and your ability to **respond** appropriately.

Your discussion could take the form of a formal debate in front of the whole class or an informal discussion in a small group. You might be discussing a real issue of worldwide importance, something that concerns your school or even an invented scenario.

Regardless of the scenario there are certain things that you should do:
- Express your points clearly and give time for your audience or group to respond.
- Listen carefully to what others say.
- Comment on the points made by others.
- Ask relevant questions.

We spend our entire lives having discussions with people and listening and responding to others. Nevertheless, in a controlled assessment situation we have to ensure that we take part in discussion effectively. It is really important that we listen sensitively and respond accordingly – we may even change previously held views.

Preparing for Discussion

As with preparing for an individual presentation, it is vital that you are familiar with your topic area. You might have different ideas from the other people that are taking part in the discussion, but you still need to have an overview of the whole topic, to be able to develop points made by others and to ask appropriate questions that will stimulate further discussion. If you are chairing the discussion, you will be expected to lead the discussion and so research and preparation are particularly important.

In order to really explore your topic it will be necessary to ask and answer a range of questions. **Open questions** are most effective – they allow the person answering to offer lots of detail and this could take the talk onto a whole new topic. 'How' and 'Why' are a good place to start!

✓ Maximise Your Marks

Getting a high grade is all about focus. You must show that you are paying attention to the task. Do not try and force a reaction – a natural response is much more animated and will show that you have been listening effectively. This will then allow you to absorb the ideas that are being discussed and react to these, encouraging interaction from others.

Drama and Role Play

The drama and role play element of your controlled assessment requires you to create a believable role or character. To do this, you will need to show **empathy** for the part that you are playing and stay in role – no giggling or slipping out of character.

There are lots of different parts that you could play: it may be that you are talking from the point of view of a character that you have been studying in class or a fictional character that you have created. Some exam boards might also want you to act out the roles of a 'real life' scenario, such as an interviewer or applicant in a job interview. To do any of this well you need to put yourself in your character's shoes and talk and behave as he or she would.

Build Your Understanding

Think about your favourite actors – what is it about them that makes you enjoy watching them? Most probably, the fact that the characters they are playing seem real to you. In order to have created a believable character, the person playing the part needs to have thought about the role in detail:

- What motivates the character?
- What attitudes and beliefs does he/she have?
- How does he/she behave on a day-to-day basis?
- What is the character's history and how has that shaped his/her character?

Searching questions like these allow you to add depth to your role – a key part of the assessment criteria. Another important feature is sustaining your role: you will do this through voice, facial expression, movement and gesture.

✓ Maximise Your Marks

Try to relate any role that you are playing to a personal experience. Do you know of anybody who has experienced something similar to any element of your performance? If it is a character that you are studying in class, make sure that you are able to convey everything that you know about them. Rehearse in front of somebody that you know will be honest and give you constructive feedback. A top-grade student will not only create a complex character that fulfils a challenging role, but will sustain the interest of the audience through the use of both verbal and non-verbal communication.

? Test Yourself

1. What three things are you being asked to demonstrate when taking part in a group discussion?

2. In order to create a believable character, what should you do?

3. Why is it a good idea to rehearse in front of someone?

4. What is an open question?

★ Stretch Yourself

1. Look at the statements below and practise saying them, thinking about your facial expression, tone of voice, gestures and movement:

   a) Your behaviour is totally unacceptable, I am going to be sending a letter home and putting you in an after school detention.

   b) Oh he/she is so good looking – every time I see them I feel like I'm going to pass out.

Studying Spoken Language

Spoken Language

We hear spoken language around us all the time. We use the spoken word to explain our feelings, convey information, interact with others, ask questions and recount events.

As part of your exam you will be expected to study spoken language in the same way that you study reading or writing. However, talk has its own conventions and ways of being analysed. In your study of spoken language you will research and investigate the following:

- **Your own language** – we all have our own individual way of talking, known as our **idiolect**.
- **Attitudes to spoken language and identity** – we all learned to speak in a similar context: with our family and during our early days in school. However, as our language skills develop, our spoken language differs greatly. The way that people speak can reveal a lot about social attitudes and relationships. Speech that varies between different groups of people in different social situations is referred to as a **sociolect**.

One of the most common features of our spoken identity occurs as a result of our **accent** and **dialect**. We often make judgments about people based on **stereotypical** ideas about accents and dialects.

- **Spoken genres** – just as books can be categorised into genres so too can speech, for example spontaneous speech, scripted speech and occupational speech.
- **Multi-modal talk** – advances in technology have allowed new ways of communication to develop. We now communicate with people by text, email, social networking sites and instant messaging.

✓ Maximise Your Marks

In order to gain a higher grade in your spoken language study, you need to be able to describe features of talk and analyse these features using the correct terminology.

Key Terms

Term	Definition
Accent	Pronunciation of words by an individual or group. Accents can be regional or social.
Dialect	Is sometimes associated with accent, but refers to the vocabulary and grammar that people use.
Standard English	The conventional use of words and grammar in the English Language.
Formal and Informal Language	Informal language is a more relaxed way of speech that we use with family and friends. Formal language is a more standard type of speech used in professional and business situations.
Transcript	Spoken language that has been written down so that it can be studied. It includes features of speech such as pauses, fillers, etc.
Pronunciation	The way that we utter words.

Transcripts

You will most probably be looking at **transcripts**. A transcript is a written record of what has been said and just like analysing a piece of poetry or prose, there are certain stylistic conventions that you have to be aware of:

- **Fillers** – words that are used to fill in pauses in conversations such as 'um' and 'er'.
- **False starts** – when you start to say one thing and then switch to another topic without finishing what you first said.
- **Repetition** – in spontaneous speech we often repeat certain words.
- **Overlap** – when people talk over each other.
- **Pauses** – short or long silences.
- **Elision** – when we leave certain letters out of certain words or when words are 'slurred' together, for example: 'wanna' instead of 'want to'.
- **Phatic language** – small talk, speech that does not have a big meaning or play a vital part in what you are saying.
- **Deixis** – language that can only be understood in the context of the conversation.

When you study a transcript it will probably resemble the example below. You will notice that there are no punctuation marks and that certain symbols are used throughout. To show a pause in speech we use (.) and if it is a slightly longer pause we put numbers in the brackets to indicate how many seconds of pause there are (3). Interruptions and overlaps are shown by the use of // at the point where the overlap takes place.

> **A:** hey (.) how's you (.) haven't seen you in ages
>
> **B:** //yeah good thanks mate (.) been really busy with school stuff (.) tryna get my head round all this English stuff (.) ready for the mock exam (1) you done much revision
>
> **A:** er not really (2) you seen this that was put up of Tommo

✓ Maximise Your Marks

When referring to any elements of dialogue in a transcript use the term 'utterance'.

Build Your Understanding

When analysing speech, there are lots of things to look and listen out for:

- What it sounds like – the accent and pronunciation might reveal the regional and social background of the person.
- The **vocabulary** used – regional dialects contain words that are common to certain areas. In Cornwall for example, you might hear somebody say, 'Where are you to?' meaning, 'Where are you?' Also, our vocabulary changes depending on whom we are talking to. You might find yourself using more formal language when talking to a teacher and more colloquial language when talking to your friends. The way that people address one another can reveal a lot about their relationship.
- **Paralinguistic features** of speech – this refers to the non-verbal elements of communication such as gestures, body language and tone of voice. This is a really important part of communication and reveals a lot about what is taking place.
- **Pragmatics** – these are the hidden or implied meanings of what people say. For example: 'It's very draughty in here' meaning 'Please close the window.'

❓ Test Yourself

1. Rearrange the letters in the anagrams below to reveal some of the stylistic conventions of speech:
   a) llersfi
   b) vapreol
   c) sixdie

★ Stretch Yourself

1. Look at the transcript in the box alongside and see if you can identify examples of:
   a) fillers   d) elision
   b) phatic speech   e) overlap
   c) dialect/slang

Studying Spoken Language

The Importance of What We Say

The way that people speak can reveal a lot about them and their identity. Through accent and dialect we are often able to detect what region a person originates from; the vocabulary and grammar they use and their pronunciation can also reveal information about their social background. However, it is important to remember that accent and dialect are not fixed. As people have begun to travel more and do not necessarily live in the same place throughout their lifetime, accents and dialects merge; this is called '**dialect levelling**'.

People also change the way that they talk depending on who they are with and where they actually are. This is called '**code switching**' and suggests that there are occasions when people are conscious about the way that they speak and the assumptions that people will make about them because of this.

People often have preconceived ideas about certain accents and dialects. People who speak using Standard English in a 'posh' accent are often assumed to be better educated or more wealthy. In advertising, research has shown that people with a Geordie accent are seen as being more friendly and people with a slight Scottish accent are considered to be trustworthy.

Build Your Understanding

Just as we have different genres in music – from hip-hop to classical – we also have different genres in speech. Speech can be spontaneous but it can also be written and rehearsed. From dialogue in a film to commentary in sport, the way that we communicate varies according to how much planning has gone into the speech. In particular, people in the public eye, such as newsreaders and politicians, spend a lot of time composing and rehearsing what they say. Politicians, in particular, really craft their talk to highlight key messages and often use a variety of rhetorical devices to make their talk sound more convincing and sincere.

Multi-Modal Talk

Multi-modal talk is exactly what it sounds like – talk that contains multiple features of both written and spoken language. These new modes of talk have occurred as a result of recent technologies such as mobile phones and the Internet. These types of spoken language are often quite short and concise so that 'chat' is brief. This is done through abbreviating words, phonetic spelling and initialisms. Multi-modal talk is often informal as it takes place between friends.

Texting

Texting is an example of multi-modal language as it combines both spoken and written language. Text speak is made up of lots of phatic language, compressed language and uses emoticons to portray feelings. Text speak often combines letters and numbers and is a non-standard form of language as it does not follow the same grammatical rules of other written modes. It does however have some common features that enable us to identify it as text language. How often do you use the following in your messages?

- Numbers and symbols instead of words: 2 (to, two, too) @ (at).
- Phonetic spelling: cul8r (see you later).
- Acronyms: LOL (laughing out loud).
- Initialisms: TMB (text me back).
- Emoticons: 0((sad face).
- Short sentences and non-standard grammar: im gd thnks how u.
- Capitalisation and exclamation marks to add emphasis: FURIOUS!!!

Texting is a popular form of communication because it is quick and cheap, but as with all forms of communication there is certain etiquette and texting does have problems as words can be ambiguous and misleading. Texting is also an informal type of language; there are occasions where it is not appropriate to text and doing so in the wrong context can be seen as rude.

Some people also believe that texting is a bad thing because it can be damaging for people's spelling and grammar. Equally, some people find texting difficult and would rather have a verbal communication; there are critics who think that texting is affecting people's ability to talk. However, it is important to remember that language is constantly evolving and, although text messaging is a relatively modern phenomenon, there have always been abbreviations, acronyms and symbols in language.

Online Talk

The Internet has also affected the way that people communicate. Emails, instant messaging, blogs, chat rooms and social network sites are all popular forms of multi-modal communication. How many of these do you use to communicate with people that you know?

Unlike text messages, emails vary in length and can be used in both formal and informal situations. You might regularly email friends and family, but a lot of business also takes place over the Internet and so you could just as easily be emailing a prospective employer or university.

Formal emails require you to use Standard English, whereas informal emails will often use similar conventions to text speak.

✓ Maximise Your Marks

For your spoken language study, you just need to remember that talk is all around you. Every minute of everyday we are presented with speech in a variety of different contexts. Choose something that you are interested in and then select examples of data to reinforce the points that you make. To get an A* you need to provide detailed analysis of any examples of speech that you collect or are given. You also need to evaluate how spoken language is adapted and comment on the reasons for this.

? Test Yourself

1. What is meant by 'dialect levelling'?
2. What is meant by the term 'code switching'?
3. What is multi-modal communication?
4. Why do people use abbreviations and emoticons in text messages and instant messages?

★ Stretch Yourself

1. Why do some people believe that texting is a 'bad' thing?

Answers

Introduction

Pages 6–7 Back to Basics
Test Yourself Answers
1. Capital letters should be used at the beginning of a new sentence, for titles, names of people, places, companies, months of the year and days of the week, etc.
2. The main types of punctuation are: full stop, comma, exclamation mark, hyphen/dash, brackets, speech marks, question mark, colon and semi-colon.
3. Grammatically correct sentences must start with a capital letter and end with a full stop. Every sentence needs at least one verb. The verb must be in the correct tense and form. Your sentence needs to make sense.
4. The basic rules of paragraphing are: start a new paragraph when there is a change of time, place, topic, person, speaker.

Stretch Yourself Answers
1. On behalf of the students of Ash Meadow, I would like to share with you our concerns about the school environment. When I say 'environment' I mean not the state of the world in general, but the surroundings in which we all work.

   We students have become very concerned about the amount of litter in the school. The corridors and classrooms are covered in all kinds of detritus: sweet wrappers, empty crisp packets and discarded drink cans. Desks are covered in offensive graffiti and their undersides studded with stale gum.

   Furthermore, in the corridors very few bins are provided and they are overflowing with litter. They are too small and too flimsy for the job. Again, there is graffiti. Our beautiful displays, into which we have put so much work, have been violated and defaced. This will not motivate the students of Ash Meadow.

   Finally, I turn to the foyer – the first impression given to any visitor. Not the warmest of welcomes. It is drab, uncared for and unfriendly. No one entering it would feel welcome. No one could leave it without a sense of relief.

   I should be most grateful if you, as Principal of Ash Meadow College, would give my points some thought. We, the students, would be only too happy to present you with our own proposals for improvement.

Pages 8–11 Writing Skills
Test Yourself Answers
1. The connective phrases that can be used include: notably, significantly, in particular, especially, obviously, clearly, above all and most importantly.
2. You use a colon before a list or quotation for example:
   I could only find three of the ingredients for flapjack: sugar, oats and syrup.
   A colon can also be used to add an explanation, for example:
   The building is very tall: it has twenty-three floors.
   You use a semi-colon to link two clauses (phrases that could stand alone as sentences) that are closely related. For example:
   Revision classes will start next week; anyone can attend.
   A semi-colon can also be used to separate items in a list, usually where each item consists of more than one word, for example:
   Twilight introduces the story of Bella, Edward and his family; New Moon looks at the love triangle between Edward, Bella and Jacob; Eclipse sees the vampires at war with the wolves; and Breaking Dawn sees the drama resolved.

Stretch Yourself Answers
1. a) practice
   b) know
   c) whether
   d) vain
   e) allowed
   f) write
   g) passed
   h) heard
   i) past
   j) practise
   k) we're

Non-Fiction

Pages 12–13 Reading Non-Fiction
Test Yourself Answers
1. P – The leaflet, aimed at parents and written by teachers, uses lots of facts and statistics to encourage parents to make their children revise:
   E – '97 per cent of students who revise thoroughly will achieve at least their predicted grade.'
   E – As this is such a high percentage, parents will be convinced of the benefits of revision and insist their children attend revision classes.

Stretch Yourself Answers
1. For practice only.

Pages 14–15 Conventions and Features
Test Yourself Answers
1. The paragraph rewritten could read:
   I confronted the man about the car that he sold me and said, 'Excuse me Sir, I recently bought a car from you and it is truly awful.'
   He had the audacity to just shrug his shoulders and reply, 'And?' I was furious at his attitude.
2. The paragraph rewritten could read:
   I went to the dining room to get my dinner. 'Hiya,' I said to my mum as we sat down at the table. 'Pass me the water, will you?'

Stretch Yourself Answers
1. These are some possible answers:
   a) Bullet points – page 12 under 'Analysing Non-Fiction'.
   b) Bold font – page 12 'Who', What' and 'Why'.
   c) Heading – page 12 'Reading Non-Fiction'.
   d) Imperative – page 13 'Test Yourself'.
   e) Illustration – image on page 13.
   f) Diagram – there are two on page 6.
   g) Icon – next to sub-headings 'Maximise Your Marks', 'Boost Your Memory', etc.
   h) Alliteration – 'Maximise Your Marks'.
   i) Rhetorical question – page 12 'What is Non-Fiction?'

Pages 16–17 Writing Techniques
Test Yourself Answers
1. a) Fact
   b) Opinion
   c) Fact
   d) Opinion
   e) Fact

Stretch Yourself Answers
1. a) List of three – '(1) unemptied bins, (2) vandalised bus shelters and (3) rat infested alleys.'
   b) Repetition – 'fellow citizens' and 'help to end'.
   c) Rhetorical question – 'Are you walking around with your eyes shut?'
   d) Direct address – 'I am appealing to you' and 'Please, help to end...'
   e) Metaphor – 'drowning in a sea of rubbish'.

Pages 18–19 Audience
Test Yourself Answers
1. a) Broadsheet
   b) Tabloid
   c) Tabloid
   d) Broadsheet
   e) Tabloid

Stretch Yourself Answers
1. To answer this question, you need to pick out key features from a text, both presentational devices and linguistic techniques, and explain how they are used to appeal specifically to the intended audience. Look back at the features covered on pages 14–19 to check if there are any you have missed.

Pages 20–21 Writing Non-Fiction
Test Yourself Answers
1. a) To **advise** the readers about their problems.
   b) To **persuade** the audience to give money and time.
   c) To **argue** the other side of the case and **persuade** readers to your point of view.
   d) To **explain** how to construct the ship.
   e) To **describe** your experience and **entertain** your readers.

Stretch Yourself Answers
1. For practice only. Your plan is likely to include:
   • An introduction
   • Main point
   • Development of main point
   • Conclusion

Pages 22–23 Writing for Difference Audiences
Test Yourself Answers
1. a) Dear Katie...Lots of love.
2. c) Dear Mrs Arbuckle...Yours sincerely.
3. d) Dear Sir...Yours faithfully.
4. b) Dear Editor...Yours faithfully.

Stretch Yourself Answers
1. a) Colloquial language might be used when addressing a friend in an informal letter or writing a text for young people, perhaps on a blog or in a magazine. It could also be used for dialogue in a work of fiction.
   b) As above, but probably for a narrower audience, who you know would understand it.
   c) Standard English is used in most forms of writing.
   d) Local dialect could be used for dialogue in a novel or play.
   e) Technical language would normally be used in a text intended for people who already have an interest in and some knowledge of the subject.

Pages 24–25 Writing to Argue
Test Yourself Answers
1. Your answer could include:
   • Uniforms are smarter
   • They are cheaper than buying designer clothes
   • They identify you as part of a school organisation
   • They prevent bullying about who is or isn't wearing designer clothes

Stretch Yourself Answers
1. Your argument should:
   • Have a powerful opening stating your viewpoint
   • Points should be well structured in a logical order
   • Discourse markers should be used to link paragraphs together
   • Counter argument should be used

Pages 26–27 Writing to Persuade
Test Yourself Answers
1. a) We were called into the office even though we had not done anything wrong.
   b) You were easily the best.
   c) I would have passed but we were given a really hard question.
   d) Lee and I saw Jodie in the precinct.
   e) Give those books to Jo and me.
   f) My friends and I went to town.
   g) Where are the shops?

Stretch Yourself Answers
1. For practice only.

Pages 28–29 Writing to Inform and Explain
Test Yourself Answers
1. b), e), c), g), d), f), a)

Stretch Yourself Answers
1. For practice only. Your article is likely to include:
   • Facts and statistics
   • Technical language
   • Experts' views
   • Connective phrases to link your ideas

Pages 30–31 Answers to Practice Questions
For each of the following questions, there are two marks awarded. The first (maximum 20) is for content, organisation and whether your answer is appropriate for the purpose and audience. The second mark (maximum 10) is for accuracy of spelling, punctuation and grammar. Tick off each of the skills that you have demonstrated and decide which mark most accurately reflects your achievement.

Your total mark (out of 30) will be roughly equivalent to the following grades:

A*	27–30	E	12–14
A	24–26	F	9–11
B	21–23	G	6–8
C	18–20	U	0–5
D	15–17		

Question 1a) and Question 2a)

Marks	Skills
16–20 Clear and successful	Clearly and concisely written. Engages the reader with detailed information. Clearly states intentions and purpose of writing. Sounds convincing. Uses formal language and Standard English throughout 1a) or an appropriate informal style 2a). Uses informative devices. Gives a variety of reasons. Paragraphs are linked effectively. Letter starts and ends appropriately (Dear Mr/Ms X..., Yours sincerely for 1a) or an informal way for 2a). Varied and adventurous vocabulary.
10–15 Mostly clear	Clearly written. A variety of reasons put forward but not always developed. Uses formal language and Standard English throughout for 1a) or appropriate informal language for 2a). States reasons for writing. Uses paragraphs. Some discursive markers used, e.g. 'Firstly'. Varied vocabulary.
1–9 Some attempts	Attempts to write a letter of application/letter to a friend. Mostly appropriate tone – aware of who the audience is. Gives some reasons about why they should be employed.
0 marks	Nothing written

Marks	Technical accuracy/quality of written communication
8–10	Grammatically accurate throughout. Almost all words (including ambitious words) spelt correctly. Range of punctuation used for effect (; : ... – !). Standard English used when appropriate. A variety of sentence forms (simple, complex, compound and fragments) used when appropriate for effect.
5–7	Most sentences are grammatically correct. Capital letters, full stops and the basic punctuation mostly used correctly. Accurate spelling of most words. Some variety in sentence structure.
1–4	Some control of grammar. Writes in sentences, which are sometimes accurately punctuated. Uses simple and some complex sentences. Words in common use spelt correctly.

Answers

Question 1b) and Question 2b)

Marks	Skills
16–20 Clear and successful	Clearly and concisely written. Engages the reader with detailed arguments and appropriate tone. Clearly focused on the purpose. Sounds convincing. Uses formal language and Standard English when appropriate. Gives a variety of reasons. Paragraphs are linked effectively. May use devices such as headings, subheadings, strap line, byline, etc. for the article 1b) or a variety of rhetorical devices for the speech 2b). Varied and adventurous vocabulary.
10–15 Mostly clear	Clearly written. A variety of reasons put forward but not always developed. Uses formal language and Standard English when appropriate. Also uses less formal language to suit the audience. Usually focused on the purpose. Uses paragraphs. Some discursive markers used, e.g. 'Firstly'. May use a limited number of presentational devices, such as headline and bullet points 1b) or rhetorical devices 2b). Varied vocabulary.
1–9 Some attempts	Attempts to write an article or speech. Appropriate tone – aware of audience. Gives some reasons about health and fitness.
0 marks	Nothing written worthy of credit.

For marks out of ten for technical accuracy, see the mark scheme for questions 1a) and 2a) on page 89.

Questions 3(a), 3(b), 4(a) and 4(b)

Marks	Skills
16–20 Clear and successful	Clearly and concisely written. Engages the reader with detailed arguments/information and appropriate tone. Clearly focused on the purpose. Sounds convincing. Uses formal language and Standard English when appropriate. Uses a range of rhetorical devices, e.g. rhetorical questions, lists of three, emotive language, anecdotes. Gives a variety of arguments. Uses counter argument. Paragraphs are linked effectively. Varied and adventurous vocabulary.
10–15 Mostly clear	Clearly written. A variety of arguments put forward but not always developed. Uses formal language and Standard English when appropriate. Also uses less formal language to suit the audience. Usually focused on the purpose. Uses paragraphs. Some discursive markers used, e.g. 'Firstly'. A limited number of rhetorical devices used. Varied vocabulary.
1–9 Some attempts	Attempts to write a speech/article/letter. Appropriate tone – aware of audience. Gives some reasons about owning/not owning a mobile phone.
0 marks	Nothing written worthy of credit.

For marks out of ten for technical accuracy, see the mark scheme for questions 1a) and 2a) on page 89.

Pages 32–33 Answers to Practice Questions

1. Award yourself a mark for each point that you make from the following list (maximum 2 marks):
   - To inform people about current events in the news.
   - To explain the chaos and havoc in London.
   - To inform people about student reaction to rising tuition fees and cuts to EMA.
   - To inform people about anti-government behaviour.
   - To inform people about how many people turned up to highlight how many people care about this issue.
   - To inform people of students' riotous behaviour.
   - To inform people about who condemned the action of the students.
   - To inform people about how the police coped with the situation.
   - To explain why students are angry.

2. Award one mark for each fact from the list below (maximum 2 marks):
   - Over 50 000 students attended.
   - 35 arrests.
   - Protesters climbed onto roofs.
   - Protesters smashed windows.
   - Protesters started fires.
   - Ratio of police to protestors was 1: 200.
   - Biggest student protest in generations.

3. Award yourself a mark for each feature (up to four) and a mark for each explanation:

Advert/splash	To encourage the reader to buy the newspaper in the first place.
Picture of protester spraying graffiti on the wall	This image is used to show some of the anti-social methods that protesters used.
Not showing the face of the protester	He is anonymous – could be anyone – his face is hidden because he is vandalising public property.
Colours	Red is used for the word 'Exclusive' to contrast with the other fonts and highlight how important this article is.
Different font sizes	The article's headline is in a bigger font to stand out and so that you can easily see what the article is about.
Capitalisation	Capitals are used for the headline and buzz word to highlight their importance.
Bold font	The first paragraph is in bold to emphasise the summary of the article.

4. Award yourself a mark for each language feature (up to four) and a mark for each explanation:

Buzz word	The word 'EXCLUSIVE' is used to suggest that this is the only paper running the story from this particular angle.
Alliteration	The writer uses alliteration in the subheading to highlight key words and draw the reader's attention to the chaos that protesters caused 'Cause Chaos'.
Headline that uses a song lyric	The article headline is a famous song lyric that we associate with anarchy / riots – it also uses the word 'we' which involves the audience.
Emotive language	Powerful and emotive language is used to highlight how angry the protesters were and how shocked people in power were by people's reactions, such as 'tension' 'growing anger' 'shocked and astounded' 'fury'.

Your total mark (out of 20) will be roughly equivalent to the following grades:

A*	18–20	E	8–9
A	16–17	F	6–7
B	14–15	G	4–5
C	12–13	U	0–3
D	10–11		

Creative Writing

Pages 34–35 Narrative Writing and Genre
Test Yourself Answers
1. a) The direct speech hook.
   b) The atmospheric hook.
   c) The question hook.

Stretch Yourself Answers
1. For practice only.

Pages 36–37 Characterisation and Imagery
Test Yourself Answers
1. Possible answers include:
   a) The moon glowed like...a firefly/torch/burning flame.
   b) Rain fell from the sky like...tears from a bleeding heart.
   c) Dewdrops glistened on the glass like...diamonds.
   d) The crows cackled like...evil witches.
   e) The road wound its way up the mountain like...a coil on a spring.
   f) The sea was...a hungry dog.
   g) Her eyes were...deep blue pools.

Stretch Yourself Answers
1. Your answer might include references to the teacher's unusual speech, and the use of the verb 'bellowed' to describe his speech. Your impression of James might be formed by his use of the phrase 'just another...' and the adverb 'sarcastically'.

Pages 38–39 Transforming Texts
Test Yourself Answers
1. For example:
   Pigs Wave Farewell to Wicked Wolf
   When a 'huff' and a 'puff' just isn't enough.

Stretch Yourself Answers
1. For practice only. Your article should:
   - Take inspiration from the original fairy tale (e.g. theme, characters, setting).
   - Follow the conventions of a newspaper article.
   - Be appropriate for the intended audience.
   - Engage the reader.
   - Use a variety of sentence structures.

Pages 40–41 Answers to Practice Questions
For each of the following questions, there are two marks awarded. The first (maximum 20) is for content, organisation and whether your answer is appropriate for the purpose and audience. The second mark (maximum 10) is for accuracy of spelling, punctuation and grammar. Tick off each of the skills that you have demonstrated and decide which mark most accurately reflects your achievement.

Your total mark (out of 30) will be roughly equivalent to the following grades:

A*	27–30	E	12–14
A	24–26	F	9–11
B	21–23	G	6–8
C	18–20	U	0–5
D	15–17		

Questions 1–4

Marks	Skills
16–20 Clear and successful	Clearly and concisely written. Engages the reader and sustains interest throughout. Imaginative and original. Paragraphs are linked effectively. Varied and adventurous vocabulary. Maintains an appropriate tone for the intended audience throughout. Convincing voice maintained throughout. May attempt to use techniques such as irony or emotive language.
10–15 Mostly clear	Clearly written. Engages the reader's interest. Some imagination shown. Uses paragraphs. Uses an appropriate tone. Some discursive markers used, e.g. 'Firstly'. Varied vocabulary.
1–9 Some attempts	Attempts to write a creative piece. Mostly appropriate tone – aware of the audience. Tone and voice not always consistent.
0 marks	Nothing written.

For marks out of ten for technical accuracy, see the mark scheme for questions 1a) and 2a) on page 89.

Shakespeare

Pages 42–43 Studying Shakespeare
Test Yourself Answers
1. a) Tragedy – main character has a fatal flaw which usually results in their death and the death of those closest to them.
   b) History – usually set in the medieval period but inspired by the social and historical context of Shakespeare's time and attempts to provide social commentary.
   c) Comedy – intertwining plots with far-fetched events, problems and conflicts resolved with marriage.

Stretch Yourself Answers
1. Your answer will depend upon the play that you are studying. Look back at page 43 to check that you have mentioned the typical elements of the genre.

Pages 44–45 Shakespeare's Use of Language
Test Yourself Answers
1. a) A pun
   b) A metaphor

Stretch Yourself Answers
1. Your answer will depend upon the play that you are studying. Look back at page 45 to check that you have correctly identified the way in which the themes are explored.

Pages 46–47 *Romeo and Juliet*
Test Yourself Answers
1. For practice only.

Stretch Yourself Answers
1. For practice only.

Pages 48–49 Writing an Essay on *Romeo and Juliet*
Test Yourself Answers
1. Some of the ideas may have been controversial because the characters, especially Romeo and Juliet, use a lot of religious language and reference, but some people in the audience would see their actions as immoral and perhaps even blasphemous.

Stretch Yourself Answers
1. For practice only.

Pages 50–51 Writing an Essay on *Romeo and Juliet*
Test Yourself Answers
1. True romantic love; sexual love (lust); unrequited love; friendship; family love and duty; Christian charity.
2. Your answer will depend upon the play you are studying.

Stretch Yourself Answers
1. For practice only.

Pages 52–53 Answers to Practice Questions
Look at both parts of your answer when awarding marks from the mark scheme below. Decide which 'band' your answer falls in and award a mark out of 30 from within that band.
Your total mark (out of 30) will be roughly equivalent to the following grades:
A* 27–30
A 24–26
B 21–23
C 18–20
D 15–17
E 12–14
F 9–11
G 6–8
U 0–5

Marks	Skills
24–30 Convincing and imaginative interpretation	You appreciate and analyse alternative interpretations, making cross references where appropriate. You develop your ideas and refer in detail to aspects of language, structure and presentation, making apt and careful comparison within and between texts. You show analytical and interpretative skill when evaluating: • the play's moral and philosophical context • significant achievements within the dramatic genre • Shakespeare's exploitation of language for dramatic, poetic and figurative effect • Shakespeare's use of dramatic conventions.
15–23 Critical response Shows insight	You give personal and critical responses to the extract which shows understanding of the ways in which meaning is conveyed. You refer to aspects of language, structure and themes to support your views. You show insight when discussing: • the nature of the play, its implications and relevance • characters, structure and stagecraft • Shakespeare's use of language.
6–14 Personal response Shows understanding	Personal response with some understanding of meaning and the ways that it is conveyed. You comment on aspects of structure, language and theme as well as expressing your views. You show understanding when discussing: • the nature of the play and its structure • the appeal of the play to an audience • Shakespeare's language.
1–5 Limited response Familiar with key themes/ ideas	Personal response with comments about key themes/ideas. Describes rather than analyses. You make inferences and deductions and identify some features of language and structure. You refer to aspects of the text when explaining your views. You show familiarity when describing: • the nature of the play, its meaning and ideas • sequence of events and variety of characters • the impact on an audience You explore dramatic conventions.

1. Points you may have included:
   - Ideas about right and wrong, loyalty, kingship and trust.
   - Duncan's noble qualities.
   - Realises that it is a heinous crime to murder their ruler especially when he is a guest in their home.
   - Knows that his deeds will come back to haunt him.
   - The imagery in the speech is dark – symbolic of his intentions.
   - Macbeth knows that it will lead him into a dark and sinful world.
   - Ambition is not a justified reason to kill.
   - This theme of ambition is developed throughout the play.
   - Soliloquy allows us to see his innermost thoughts – we see inside the mind of a man in turmoil.
   - As the soliloquy ends it seems that he has resolved not to kill Duncan – good man at heart – however, his wife arrives and convinces him otherwise.
   - His decision to kill the King is the trigger for the rest of the play's dark actions.

2. Points you may have included:
   - What has just happened – who are the characters involved.
   - Their family feud.
   - How quickly they have developed feelings for one another.
   - This is the happiest scene in the play.
   - The importance of night and day.
   - The metaphorical language.
   - The power of language.
   - Juliet questions why Romeo must be the son of her enemy.
   - She refuses to believe that Romeo is defined by being a Montague.
   - Their love prevents fear.
   - The impact that this exchange has on the rest of the play.

Drama

Pages 54–55 Studying Drama
Test Yourself Answers
1. Possible answers include: stagecraft, characterisation, plot and structure.
2. Stage directions are a set of instructions to the director and actors. They give information about setting and props.

Stretch Yourself Answers
1. Your answer will depend upon the play you are studying.
2. Your answer will depend upon the play you are studying.

Pages 56–57 Character and Audience
Test Yourself Answers
1. A sudden turn of events in a piece of drama is called coup de theatre.
2. Your answer will depend upon the play you are studying.
3. Subtext is the underlying messages and themes of the play.

Stretch Yourself Answers
1. Your answers will depend upon the play you are studying.

Pages 58–59 Analysing a Moving Image
Test Yourself Answers
1. Possible answers:

Denotation	Connotation
Glasses	Geeky
Sunglasses	Cool
Rose	Romance
Sun	Happiness
Leaf	Nature

Stretch Yourself Answers
1. For practice only.

Pages 60–61 Analysing a Moving Image
Test Yourself Answers
1. a) A long shot.
   b) A close up.
   c) An aerial shot.
   d) A moving subject shot.
   e) An extreme close up

Stretch Yourself Answers
1. For practice only.

Pages 62–63 Answers to Practice Questions
The mark scheme below applies to all questions. When awarding yourself marks from the mark scheme decide which 'band' your answer falls in and award a mark (out of 20) from within that band.

Your total mark (out of 20) will be roughly equivalent to the following grades:

A*	18–20	E	8–9
A	16–17	F	6–7
B	14–15	G	4–5
C	12–13	U	0–3
D	10–11		

Marks	Skills
15–20	You explore the role of the character within the play with insight. You focus on how the character develops and any changes that they undergo. Close analysis of detail – uses cleverly chosen quotes to support points made. Comments on the playwright's use of language/structure/form/stagecraft and the effect that these have on the audience. Essay is very well written – technically accurate throughout. Uses a combination of P.E.E. paragraphs and embeds quotations into writing.
10–14	You offer a considered analysis of character. You focus on key events that include the character. Uses quotations from the text to back up points made. Comments on the writer's choice of language. Explores key themes/ideas/settings/relationships and how these link to the character. Essay is well written – spelling and grammar is generally accurate. Uses P.E.E. paragraphs.
5–9	You offer a sustained response to the task. Understands the role played by the character. Uses detail to support points being made. Can identify some of the effects of the writer's choice of language. Awareness of ideas/themes/settings. Quality of writing is sufficient – clearly conveys meaning – some errors with spelling/paragraphing/expression.
1–4	Familiar with the character. Retells the story referring to the character and the role that they play. Narrative rather than analytical. Makes generalisations about themes/ideas/settings/relationships. Frequent errors in spelling and grammar.

1. An Inspector Calls
Points you may have included:
- The inspector is a figure of authority
- He is confident, intelligent and probing but can get impatient with the witnesses
- Socially he is from a lower class than the Birlings and they (especially Mr Birling) expect him to be polite and deferent
- He is not impressed or intimidated by them
- He is a figure of mystery – why would a police inspector investigate a suicide?
- He seems to know more about the other characters than he might be expected to know
- His arrival acts as an 'instigating incident' and punctures the cosy world of the Birlings
- Is there any significance in his name?
- Is he a 'ghost from the future'?
- At the end he warns of what will happen if things do not change and he gives us the message that we are all responsible for each other

2. Kindertransport
Points you may have included:
- The play opens with three generations of women who seem to have comfortable lives and conventional relationships
- There may be some tension between Faith and Evelyn
- The effect of Faith's discovery of her mother's past
- The presentation of Eva and Helga in Germany and its juxtaposition with 'present day' scenes
- Helga's sacrifice in letting go of Eva
- The contrast between Lil and Helga
- The impact of history on individuals – what made Eva change into Evelyn?
- Issues of nature and nurture
- The complexity of Eva/Evelyn's relationship with her two mothers
- What the play tells us about identity and culture through parent/child relationships

3. The Crucible
Points you may have included:
- John Proctor is a respected and influential figure in Salem
- When he first appears the other characters listen to him

- He has clearly been in dispute with Parris
- We learn of his weakness in having a relationship with Abigail
- In the second act we are given a picture of a marriage under strain – Elizabeth and John love each other but are not comfortable together any more
- John is outspoken and courageous in denouncing the girls
- Other characters look to him for leadership
- He is at the centre of a terrible moral dilemma
- He seems willing to compromise his principles at the end but cannot perform the symbolic act of signing his name to a lie
- He could be seen as a tragic hero but at the same time he is an 'everyman' figure

4. Blood Brothers
Points you may have included:
- At the beginning the story is seen mainly from Mrs Johnstone's point of view
- The narrator introduces us to her and helps us to become sympathetic towards her
- She is presented as a hard-working, well-meaning woman who is doing her best to bring up her children
- We are also reminded of what she was like when she was young and full of hope
- Mrs Lyons might initially seem less sympathetic – she is middle class and quite wealthy in contrast with Mrs Johnstone
- However, she is desperate to have a baby, which makes her anxious and rather neurotic, inspiring some sympathy
- The audience might well lose sympathy for her after she does her 'deal' with Mrs Johnstone
- There is a contrast in the way the two mothers bring up their sons – think about in what ways they might be seen as 'good' or 'bad' mothers
- Eddie and Mickey turn out very differently because of the opportunities they are given
- Why does it end tragically? How far is it because of the mothers' actions and how far because of their environment and society?
- The impact of the opening and closing scenes on the audience's attitude to the two characters

Prose

Pages 64–65 Novels and Short Stories
Test Yourself Answers
1. We learn that Pip is the only surviving child of his parents, the others having died very young. We also learn that his parents died when he was very young, so that he barely knew them. He is being brought up by his Aunt, who is married to the blacksmith Joe Gargery, in the marshlands.
2. The setting is a cemetery. It is dark and bleak. Beyond the cemetery are the marshes.

Stretch Yourself Answers
1. You might have said that the use of the first person narrative engages the reader immediately and vividly with the character of Pip; that we feel engaged by his personality; and that we feel empathy for him.

Pages 66–67 Literary Techniques
Test Yourself Answers
1. These are some possible examples you may have found.
   a) Repetition – 'Pip... Pip... Pip'.
   b) Dialogue – most of the last section, beginning 'Hold your noise'.
   c) Powerful adjectives – 'raw... savage... terrible'.
   d) Alliteration – 'glared and growled'.
   e) Personification – 'lamed by stones... torn by briars'.

Stretch Yourself Answers
1. The main difference is that Pip speaks in Standard English and the stranger does not. The way his speech is written suggests an accent (probably from London). This shows a difference in social class and experience and perhaps emphasises the roughness of the stranger and the potential threat he presents to the well-mannered, polite Pip.

Pages 68–69 Exploring Culture in Prose
Test Yourself Answers
1. The term 'multicultural society' means a society made up of several cultures.
2. You may have commented on the way in which food is eaten 'where we ate food with our fingers', the difference in manners 'where manners were so courtly that a raised eyebrow could imply an insult', the difference in sensibilities 'where sensibilities were so finely tuned that an advert featuring a woman in a bikini could clear a room'.

Stretch Yourself Answers

1. Your answer will depend upon the text you are studying.

Pages 70–71 Culture in *Of Mice and Men*
Test Yourself Answers

1. Steinbeck does not give Curley's wife a name because her anonymity highlights how insignificant she is. She is merely 'another woman' living in a man's world.

2. The significance of the novel starting and ending at the same place is that it can be seen as a reminder of the timelessness and supremacy of nature – our natural world has to endure human life and the trouble that we bring to it.

Stretch Yourself Answers

1. Your answer will depend upon the text you are studying.

Pages 72–73 Answers to Practice Questions

The mark scheme below applies to all questions. When awarding yourself marks from the mark scheme decide which 'band' your answer falls in and award a mark out of 20 from within that band.

Your total mark (out of 20) will be roughly equivalent to the following grades:

A* 18–20   E 8–9
A 16–17   F 6–7
B 14–15   G 4–5
C 12–13   U 0–3
D 10–11

Questions 1–3

Marks	Skills
15–20	A perceptive exploration and evaluation of extract. Understands its relevance and makes wider links to the rest of the novel. Understands the social/historical/cultural context of the text. Sensitively explores the significance of the writer's choice of language, structure and form. Thoughtful response that is engaging to read. Essay is very well written – technically accurate throughout. Uses a combination of P.E.E. paragraphs and embeds quotations into writing.
10–14	Attempts to explore and explain links between the chosen text and the rest of the novel. Comments on social/historical/cultural context. Is able to analyse the chosen section in detail. Offers an insight into the writer's choice of language, structure and form. Essay is well written – spelling and grammar is generally accurate. Uses P.E.E. paragraphs.
5–9	Some understanding of links between the chosen text and the rest of the novel. Understanding of some features of language, structure and form. Quality of writing is sufficient – clearly conveys meaning – some errors with spelling/paragraphing/expression.
1-4	Some simple comments made about a key event. Mostly descriptive – retells story/plot. Limited awareness of language/structure and form. Quality of writing is sufficient – clearly conveys meaning – some errors with spelling/paragraphing/expression.

1. *Pride and Prejudice*

Points you may have included:

- Elizabeth thinks she understands Darcy's character although she has known him for a very short time
- According to her he thinks he has no faults
- He says he strives to avoid weaknesses such as vanity or pride but her smile indicates that she thinks he is guilty of these faults
- He does admit that he can be unforgiving
- His account of his own character, in contrast with Elizabeth's assumptions, shows that he is self-aware
- Although he appears to be talking quite seriously, by putting up with Elizabeth's 'examination' he shows that he is tolerant and not as 'proud' as she thinks
- His last remark shows that perhaps he is more perceptive than Elizabeth and understands her better than she understands him
- His smile can be interpreted in several ways. Is he amused by Elizabeth, impressed by her or is the smile patronising and/or ironic?

2. *Of Mice and Men*

Points you may have included:

- She is important because her murder is the climax of the story
- Although she is the victim of the crime, George and Lenny are also victims
- It is their tragedy as much as (or more than) hers
- She is the only woman in the novel and could be seen to represent the role and experience of women in society
- Like many of the of the characters she has dreams and ambitions that have been shattered
- While she is not a pleasant character, readers might still have sympathy for her
- She does not have a name, being always referred to as 'Curley's wife'
- This makes her seem marginalised and without a real identity

3. *To Kill a Mockingbird*

Points you may have included:

- The story is told by his daughter, Scout
- Therefore, he is seen primarily as a father
- The relationship is very close, particularly because the mother is dead
- Scout 'hero worships' Atticus
- As an adult, looking back on her childhood, she continues to do this: she has nothing negative to say about him
- She sees him as a hero initially because of the way he behaves towards his children and neighbours
- As the case progresses she comes to realise that his actions are seen in different ways by different members of society
- There is no doubt in her mind that he is a man of integrity and a brave man
- The reader is expected to share the narrator's evaluation of Atticus

Poetry

Pages 74–75 Poetic Form and Features
Test Yourself Answers

1. a) Alliteration
   b) Personification
   c) Simile
   d) Metaphor

Stretch Yourself Answers

1. You might have noticed that the end-stop at the end of the first line gives the impression that a definitive statement has been made. The next few lines will explore this sentiment. The use of caesuras makes us stop unexpectedly, perhaps to pause for thought, or perhaps it gives the impression that the poet is stopping to think, working it out as he writes. Enjambment suggests a continuing idea or sentiment. Perhaps the poet is getting 'carried away' with an idea and does not want to pause for breath.

Pages 76–77 Poetry Comparison
Test Yourself Answers

1. Possible answers include: story, theme, form, structure, language, imagery, character, setting and voice.

2. Possible answers include: in the same way, similarly, also, just as.

Stretch Yourself Answers

1. Your answer will depend upon the poems you are studying.

Pages 78–79 Answers to Practice Questions

When awarding yourself marks from the mark scheme decide which 'band' your answer falls in and award a mark out of 20 from within that band.

Your total mark (out of 20) will be roughly equivalent to the following grades:

A* 18–20   E 8–9
A 16–17   F 6–7
B 14–15   G 4–5
C 12–13   U 0–3
D 10–11

Questions 1 and 2

Marks	Skills
15–20	A sophisticated and perceptive response. Detailed evaluation of key ideas from the poem. Well selected quotations. Understanding of the poet's choice of language, structure and form. Response is very well written – technically accurate throughout. Uses a combination of P.E.E. paragraphs and embeds quotations into writing.
10–14	A clear and sustained response. Relevant references made about key ideas within the poem. Clear understanding of the poet's choice of language, structure and form. Range of quotations. Response is well written – spelling and grammar is generally accurate. Uses P.E.E. paragraphs.
1–9	A reasonably organised response to the poem. Understanding of the story within the poem. Some reference to features of language, structure and form. Quality of writing is sufficient – clearly conveys meaning – some errors with spelling/paragraphing/expression.

1. Points you may have included:
- The repetition of 'no'
- The general sense of negativity conveyed
- The dullness of the weather
- The way in which nothing can be seen because of fog
- The way general everyday life, and especially social life, seems to stop
- The way in which the poet starts by writing about the weather, moves on to talking about people, and then returns to nature and the weather
- The use of rhyme and alliteration
- The humorous tone of the poem – in spite of the fact that he is talking about a depressing experience

2. Points you may have included about 'Dulce et Decorum est':
- The poet is writing about one horrific experience of war
- The poem is very personal, the poet being a witness to events
- The gas attack is described in accurate detail
- The poem focuses on ordinary soldiers and their experiences
- The use of vivid imagery, including metaphors and similes, to convey the experience
- The change of mood from the slow marching and trudging to excitement and panic
- The change of tense in the second half of the poem as the poet tells us how he can still see the awful scenes
- The poet's disgust and anger
- His rejection of 'the old lie'

Comparison with another poem of your choice should include consideration of:
- Content and themes
- The poet's attitude and ideas
- Tone and atmosphere
- Language
- Form and structure

Speaking and Listening

Pages 80–81 Presenting Information and Ideas
Test Yourself Answers
1. Possible answers include: cue cards, props and PowerPoint slides.

Stretch Yourself Answers
1. For practice only.

Pages 82–83 Group Discussion and Drama
Test Yourself Answers
1. Your ability to communicate your ideas, your ability to listen to what others have said and then your ability to respond appropriately.
2. Use empathy and put yourself in their shoes.
3. It is a good idea to rehearse in front of someone so that you can get honest and constructive feedback.
4. An open question will allow the person responding to provide a detailed response.

Stretch Yourself Answers
1. For practice only.

Pages 84–85 Studying Spoken Language
Test Yourself Answers
1. a) fillers
   b) overlap
   c) deixis

Stretch Yourself Answers
1. a) fillers – 'er'
   b) phatic speech – 'hey', 'yeah'.
   c) dialect/slang – 'you seen', 'you done', 'how's you'
   d) elision – 'tryna'
   e) overlap – 'yeah'

Pages 86–87 Studying Spoken Language
Test Yourself Answers
1. When accents and dialects merge as a result of people moving around from place to place.
2. When people alter the way that they talk depending on where they are and who they are with.
3. Talk that contains multiple features of both written and spoken language.
4. Because they keep the message short and cheap – also they show emotion which can be hard in a text message.

Stretch Yourself Answers
1. Some people believe that texting is a 'bad' thing because it encourages people to make spelling and grammatical errors. Others might say that it is easy to misinterpret the tone of what is said, or that it encourages bad manners (e.g. answering texts during a conversation or meeting).

Index